18
Common
Sense
Rules for
Enjoying a
Successful
Retirement

Ron Dickinson

CPA • CFP • MPA - Tax

Published by: Ron Dickinson
Editing and layout by: Teclarity, ww.teclarity.com
Cover design by: DARMEDIA, Inc.

September 2007
First edition
ISBN-10: 1533218218
ISBN-13: 978-1533218216

This book is a common sense guide to personal finance. In practical advice books, as in life, there are no guarantees, and readers are cautioned to rely on their own judgment about their individual circumstances and to act accordingly. Readers are also reminded that this book is intended for informational purposes only and is not meant to take the place of professional advice. The laws in this area are complex and constantly changing. You should consult with an experienced professional to apply the relevant laws in your state to your unique situation.

To my wife
and
soul mate,
Beverly

Special thanks to coach Rob Brown,
Founder, Encore Partners

-
-
-
-
-
-

Foreword

Retirement planning should not be overly complicated. At the same time there are no quick-fix solutions. The recipe for a successful retirement requires discipline, honesty and common sense.

Discipline means establishing a plan and sticking with it. Whether you're implementing a savings strategy to retire early or an investment withdrawal plan to support your lifestyle, you cannot jump around. Some of the best retirements are ruined when plans are unwisely changed mid-course.

Honesty means you understand both your possibilities and your limitations. You live your dreams without undermining your security. To successfully retire you must be honest with yourself and work with someone who will keep you on track.

Common sense is the final element of a successful retirement. It means you avoid quick fixes. You rely on proven strategies. You realize that when something appears too good to be true, it probably is.

This book contains all three of these key ingredients for a successful retirement – discipline, honesty, and common sense. It is written with the care and compassion the author, Ron Dickinson, has delivered to his real-life clients for the past 20 years. Whether you're planning for or living in your retirement years, you'll enjoy this easy to read guide.

Ron shows you how he has applied financial discipline in his own life as well as in the many plans he has created for his clients. He doesn't hold any punches when it comes to dispelling some of today's unscrupulous retirement planning schemes. He teaches you techniques and concepts that have stood the test of time. And he does it all with the integrity and common sense of someone who truly wants you to enjoy retirement success.

I have been in the financial services industry for over 23 years. My roles have included advising clients on retirement planning issues and teaching advisors how to build retirement planning practices. This book contains some of the best advice you will ever receive.

Enjoy!

Rob Brown
Founder
EncoreAdvisor.com

About the Author

Never trade who you are for what you want.
- Ron Dickinson

Ron Dickinson is a Financial Planner and CPA with over 20 years of experience serving the tax, financial planning and investment needs of hundreds of clients. His goal is to help each client achieve a well-balanced, successful retirement. His company's mission is "**Turning your retirement dreams into reality through proven, time tested investment solutions.**"

Ron founded Dickinson Investment Advisors with a commitment to building one-on-one relationships with each and every client. Client loyalty is established through a proven trust in Ron and his staff, personal communication with frequent updates and results that bring success.

Dickinson Investment Advisors helps clients managing their IRAs, rollovers and other retirement plan assets. Small business clients receive help in converting the intangible value of their business and real estate into significant retirement assets.

Many clients come with scattered investments that have been haphazardly accumulated over time. Ron and his team adjust these investments to help clients meet their long-term goals and commit to ongoing updates.

There are no hidden fees or charges. By incorporating a single, fee-based approach to investment and financial planning, clients receive a high level of service and advice at a reasonable price.

Complex financial concepts are explained in terms that clients understand and appreciate. The more educated the client is, the better they can participate in the creation of an investment program that considers both their tax and financial needs.

A Trademark of Dickinson Investment Advisors is open, honest and frequent communication. The value of Ron's name and how others think about his integrity is more important to him than short term profits. Many of his clients have been with him for more than 20 years. Ron strives to use only highly ranked mutual funds, top quality stocks and investment grade bonds to build diversified client portfolios that, over time, have tended to meet or exceed overall market returns.

Ron is committed to a lifetime of continuous improvement and education. In addition to a college degree in business, Ron earned a master's degree in taxation. Ron passed the rigorous CPA exam on his first attempt prior to graduating from college. Ron has also spent three years undergoing a college level concentrated study in financial planning. Ron continues to hold licenses as both a CPA and CFP (CERTIFIED FINANCIAL PLANNER™) which requires 40 to 60 hours of continuing education each year.

Family is the most important priority for Ron, and a majority of his time outside the office is spent with his wife, Bev, and their three sons. Ron and Bev are blessed with a biological son, Matthew, and two sons adopted from Korea, Philip and Andrew.

Ron is the principal owner of Dickinson Investment Advisors. He is also a shareholder in the firm of Dickinson & Clark CPAs, PC. He works primarily in financial planning and consulting for individuals and small businesses.

Ron has a bachelor's degree in accounting from Hastings College and a master's degree in taxation from the University of Texas. Before starting his CPA firm, he worked for the international accounting firm of Touche Ross & Co. Ron is actively involved as an Elder of First Christian Church in Council Bluffs, Iowa.

Professional Designations

CPA/PFS	Certified Public Accountant/ Personal Financial Planning Specialist
CFP	Certified Financial Planner
MPA	Master's in Public Accounting/Tax

Memberships

- Society of Financial Professionals
- American Institute of Certified Public Accountants
- Nebraska Society of Certified Public Accountants
- Iowa Society of Certified Public Accountants
- Licensed as a CPA in Iowa and Nebraska
- Chamber Executive Board Member of Council Bluffs Chamber of Commerce

Table of Contents

No hype, just common sense advice!

I never did a day's work in my life. It was all fun.
- Thomas Alva Edison

This is not just another book on retirement planning; it's a book about living successfully during your retirement. You won't find a bunch of confusing numbers and statistics. I won't try to frighten you. My goal is to give you a common sense tool that will help you realize your dreams and aspirations. After all, a successful retirement is so much more than money.

But let's be honest, it's truly difficult to live life to its fullest when your bank account is on empty. You need to have a full tank, so you can explore the more important things in life. Things like relationships with your spouse, kids and grandkids. Like a rewarding spiritual life. Like being able to live in a nice house with no debt and being able to golf and travel when you like. Life is no fun if you're counting pennies until your next Social Security check arrives.

My name is Ron Dickinson. I have had the good fortune of building a successful CPA firm and a growing investment management firm. My career has been a lot of fun and a great deal of hard work. But in many ways I've learned the most by observing human behavior; literally witnessing the subtle differences between retirees who are satisfied with their lives and those who are not. For more than twenty years, I have studied the traits and habits of hundreds of folks as they plan and live their retirements. For the most part, the biggest difference between financial success and failure is the use of common sense in applying basic money management principles.

Over the last couple of decades, I've had a ringside seat to watch the explosion of the financial services industry. Banks, brokerage firms, accounting practices and insurance companies all want to help plan your retirement. As more and more players have joined the retirement planning industry, the choices have become even more confusing. In doing tax returns, I have had an inside look at how all these institutions operate. The results have been both exceptional and disastrous. Generally speaking, those who have done well for their clients and whose clients seem to be the most content, have used the same common sense approach I espouse in this book.

Not only do I work hard at understanding how the financial world works, I also like to put it all into terms that the average person can understand. Life doesn't have to be complicated, but some people sure try hard to make it that way.

3

One of my pet peeves is watching financial professionals make things sound overly-complicated. They want to make themselves look smart. To me a true advisor, as opposed to a slick salesman, is someone who can boil key concepts down into easily understandable ideas. In turn, the client can think for themselves and truly express their needs and feelings. Together they can then make the best client-focused decisions possible.

I prefer to be an optimist. Unfortunately, in this journey we call life, there are obstacles that can temporarily derail even the best-laid plans. Simply hoping bad things won't happen is never a good solution. You can't just stick your head in the sand. Fortunately, most of these hazards can be avoided or overcome with common sense planning. We need to break through our bad habits and behaviors and truly believe that we deserve to live a successful retirement.

This book contains the most important concepts I teach my clients everyday. In the interest of making it user-friendly, I have excluded some of the nitty-gritty details. My belief is that if I can help you understand the big picture, you too will be able to apply the common sense principles of living a successful retirement. And that is how you will achieve your goals and aspirations.

Rule 1

What are your unique priorities?

The purpose of life is to live it, to taste experience to the utmost, to reach out eagerly and without fear for newer and richer experience.
- Eleanor Roosevelt

Priorities come in many different shapes and sizes. As you plan for a successful retirement, you need to build your financial future around your unique desires. What may be important for me as a financial counselor may not even make your top twenty list. This is one of the reasons I find my work both exciting and fun. No two investors are the same; my reward comes from helping folks understand their priorities and achieving their goals.

When I think about my own goals, my first priority is a successful and rewarding retirement with my wife. We want to get the most out of our golden years. A secondary concern is transferring our wealth to our children after we're gone. In doing this, we want to have a strong cash flow, maximize our investment flexibility and minimize taxes. Charity also plays an important role in these priorities. We currently give 10% of our earnings to charity and have charitable plans for some of our assets when we pass away. One of my core values is being generous; it helps frame my priorities.

Please don't get me wrong, I'm not suggesting you forget about your kids. In my case, I want my kids to have a great life but my job is to raise them with strong values, get them through college and position them to be productive citizens in society. Once I'm done, their job is to set their own priorities and make their own way. I'm not sure I'd really be doing them a favor by enriching them beyond giving them a great start and occasional gifts. I don't have a responsibility to build an estate to make their life comfortable at the expense of my own retirement.

Put first things first!
I find that many advisors think of retirement and estate planning in reverse order. They push fancy solutions that concentrate on doing things with your money after you're gone. They imply that your lifetime needs may need to take a backseat to your after-life needs. You have to wonder if these advisors are putting a commission ahead of your

personal well-being. But for most of us, it's more logical to put a successful retirement first.

By the way, you'll see later in these writings that I believe in efficiently passing your wealth onto children or charities, especially with money you have that exceeds your first level goals. I sometimes refer to this as "never use money." If you have "never use money" there are powerful techniques you can use to leverage those assets for your children or favorite charity.

How long will your retirement last?

Think of it another way. Most of us work several decades to accumulate our savings and investments – our wealth. We should have a chance to enjoy the fruits of our labor. After all, the average person retiring at the age of 65 will spend more than 20 years in retirement. This is an example of what I mean by common sense planning.

As you set your own priorities, keep this concept in mind. Not everyone's priorities are the same, but you still need to put first things first. Planning a successful retirement is a lot like running a business; when you develop long-term strategies you increase your chances of success. Of course, this doesn't mean you should ignore your later priorities. In fact, as I counsel individual clients, I look for solutions that provide flexibility. None of us can predict the future with absolute certainty.

Do you want it all?

Most of us can't have it all; we have competing interests. Some folks say they'll work as long as they can, while others want to retire early. Some folks want a guaranteed monthly income, while others would rather maintain large cash balances in their bank accounts. Some folks want lots of "stuff" like cars, boats and vacations, while others worry about nursing home costs. Some folks want to see their grandchildren enjoy their inheritance while they're still alive, while others want to leave major gifts to their alma maters.

On a personal level, I've never found contentment in the idea of trying to have it all. It's a losing proposition. I find satisfaction in knowing I won't run out of money even if I have to revise my desires and live a simpler life. I look more toward the intangible things in life found in meaningful relationships and good health. There are so many ways to spend and invest your money; you have to decide what is most important to you.

Your priorities are unique.

As you plan for a successful retirement, you need to build your financial future around your unique desires. Don't subject yourself to a cookie cutter approach. Find a good advisor who will help you establish your priorities and apply common sense to this critical stage of your life.

Rule 2

Is a successful retirement really just a number?

You have to learn the rules of the game. And then you have to play better than anyone else.
– Albert Einstein

Money is like a sixth sense without which you cannot make a complete use of the other five.
- W. Somerset Maugham

No, I'm not talking about your phone number or even your favorite lottery picks. I'm talking about how much money you'll need to have in savings and investments to truly enjoy your retirement. Your number is your total nest egg; you'll use it to generate a level of income that supports your ambitions. After all, a successful retirement is supposed to be fun. You get to do the stuff you've dreamed of for years. It's the culmination of a lot of hard work and successful planning.

By the way, a lot of slick salespeople will try to scare you with talk of "your number." They say things like, "You want to be sure you don't run out of money before you run out of time." And though this is definitely true, you don't need to plan or live your retirement in fear. When you understand your number and how it supports your goals, you won't need to keep looking over your shoulder in terror.

How do you come up with your number?
I spend a lot of time helping my clients answer this question. Each situation is unique, but here's how you can get a rough idea. You actually back your way into your number by first understanding your income needs. Look at your pay stubs, Social Security payments, pension income and other reliable sources of income. How much money comes in each month?

This is a great place to start because even without a detailed budget it shows you what you're spending each month. Some people say you won't need all this during retirement. They say something like "use 80% of your income as a guide" – that's rubbish. They're just trying to make you feel better. I want you to have a great retirement. I want you to be able to travel, play, enjoy your family and be charitable.

Plus, on the more serious side of things, medical costs are impossible to predict. And when your income is more fixed, the rising prices of everyday necessities can be public enemy number one. When you're calculating your number, use at least 100% of your current spending. If possible, you may even want to increase this number another ten to twenty percent.

Once you decide how much income you need each month, it's time to figure out how you plan to make it happen. Start by taking your total monthly income need and subtracting pension income, Social Security payments and other guaranteed sources of income. Whatever portion of your need that's left over will have to be generated by savings and investments.

A simple math lesson
Let's look at a simplified example by assuming you're already retired. If your after-tax income need is $5,000 per month and you have $1,500 coming in from reliable sources of income, then you'll need your nest egg to produce $3,500 a month or $42,000 a year in income.

So the question becomes: How much money will you need to produce $42,000 per year in investment income? Next, you need to estimate a rate of return; I like to assume five percent. To avoid complicated mathematical formulas and terms, simply multiply $42,000 times 20. Your answer is $840,000. In other words, you would need $840,000 in income to generate $3,500 in monthly income ($840,000 multiplied by five percent is $42,000 per year or $3,500 per month). Your number is $840,000.

For those of you who are more mathematically inclined, here's a slightly more detailed look at the calculations. You can also experiment with your own numbers.

Steps	Our Example	Try Your Own Numbers
Start with Your After-Tax Monthly Income Need	$3,500	
Multiply By 12 To Estimate Your Annual Requirement	12	
You Get Your Annual After-Tax income	$42,000	
Multiply By Your Return Factor (The Reciprocal of Your Assumed Rate of Return)	20 ($5\% = 100/5 = 20$)	
Equals Your Number	$840,000	

Warning, warning, warning – don't stop here!!!
The example above is overly simplified, but it's a great way to eyeball your retirement nest egg needs. Your actual number could be higher or lower because there are a number of other factors that could play in to your calculation. Here are a few of the most important:

- **If you're not retired yet, inflation will affect your monthly income need.**
  Look at what you need today and increase it by an inflation factor of three percent for each year between now and your estimated retirement date. So if you're ten years away from retirement that $5,000 number we used above is going to be $6,750.
- **This formula works only if your reliable sources of income will increase with inflation.**
  In other words, your pension, Social Security and other forms of guaranteed income will have to receive annual cost of living adjustments. Some do and some don't, so you need to check them out.
- **Don't forget taxes.**
  The numbers above were after tax. Uncle Sam won't forget about you when you're retired, so you'll need to factor taxes into your expenses.

Your number is extremely important; you need to be careful when you make your calculations. That's why a lot of my clients learn how to do their own estimates, but come to me to verify their results. In turn, I use some very powerful software to simulate a number of different scenarios.

Calculating your number is not an exact science, but it helps you set a target. Your target could be a number you're shooting for before retirement. Or it could be a reality check if you're already retired. I recheck my clients' numbers each time we do an annual review. It is one of the many tools we use to stay on track for a successful retirement.

Why only a 5% return?
At this point you might be wondering why I only use a five percent return assumption. After all, stocks average more than ten percent per year. And that's a great point! But, just like when you're working, you need to earn more than you spend. This allows you to give yourself a raise each year. You need to avoid a fixed income squeeze.

Think about it this way. If you had your entire nest egg in stocks and you assume an historical rate of return, you would average about ten percent per year (Don't forget, stocks aren't appropriate for everyone). If we subtract the five percent you withdraw each year, you're left with an additional five percent to cover raises and other surprises. Of that five percent, you'll probably need about three percent for inflation protection. You're left with around two percent which is a good cushion against stock market volatility.

Why would you need a cushion? Even the best money managers have to suffer through lousy years in the market. If you put any piece of your nest egg in stocks, you could be subject to down years. When stocks are down, you'll still need to draw income. I'm not going to go into the mechanics of how all this works, but believe me, you need some cushion. So five percent for you, plus three percent so you can have a raise next year, plus two percent for market volatility gives you 10%.

Small changes can make big differences.
Now that you've read through the last few paragraphs, your view on a five percent withdrawal rate may have flip-flopped. You could be wondering if five percent is too much. To be more conservative, some advisors suggest using a four percent withdrawal rate. In the calculations above, this would change your return factor from 20 to 25. To generate $3,500 in monthly income, your number would increase from $840,000 to $1,050,000.

Still other advisors suggest a more aggressive six percent withdrawal rate. This moves your return factor down from 20 to 17. A $3,500 monthly income goal would set your number at $714,000.

I like using five percent. It has proven to be a solid baseline as long as my clients and I keep monitoring their financial situations and allow for flexibility.

A successful retirement requires a good number.

As you can see from the totals above, small changes in your return factor assumption can make a huge difference in your ultimate number. After all, setting a goal of $1,050,000 is a lot harder than setting a goal of $714,000. Reaching your number could mean several more years of work, taking bigger risks in your retirement portfolio or reducing your income needs. These are all tough options to consider.

And this is where the help of a financial professional can really comes into play in achieving a successful retirement. Figuring out your number is pretty easy. The math is relatively simple. But being sure your number accurately reflects your dreams, your ability to handle risk and your need to be flexible requires constant care.

Rule 3
Inflation and taxes are a fact of life!

Inflation is when you pay fifteen dollars for the ten-dollar haircut you used to get for five dollars when you had hair.
- Sam Ewing

The hardest thing in the world to understand is the income tax.
– Albert Einstein

Over time, inflation has averaged around three percent per year. Three percent doesn't seem like much, does it? After all, that's just a few pennies out of a dollar. Well, let me tell you a story...

A frog in hot water
Inflation is like the proverbial frog in hot water. It's said that if you were to place a frog into a pot

of boiling water, it would simply jump out. But if you place a frog into a pot of warm water and slowly increase the temperature by one degree every few minutes, the frog would not be alerted to the need to jump out until it was too late.

As you plan for a successful retirement, don't think like a frog. Be alert to the dangers of inflation. Don't let it surprise you when you can least afford to do something about it. Most individuals don't want to have a surprise after they have retired and can no longer earn a living.

Whether you think about it or not, inflation slowly chips away at the spending power of your savings and investments. You need your retirement nest egg to increase by more than the rate of inflation each year.

Think back to the first house you ever purchased. There is a good chance that a new car today will cost more than your original house. If you stop to think about that one simple fact for a moment, it's astonishing. If you're at the beginning of your retirement, you'll probably need your nest egg to last longer than the time that has passed between now and the purchase of that first house. You need the wealth you've accumulated for retirement to grow faster than the rate of inflation.

Taxes turn the "heat" up even more.
Taxes can be a further drag on the buying power

of your retirement dollars. It's not uncommon to pay between 20 and 30 percent of the earnings on your investments to the federal and state governments in taxes.

Let's look at a simple example by assuming a tax rate of 25 percent on a $100,000 certificate of deposit (CD) paying you 5 percent.

The interest you earn at 5% - "Gross Return"	$5,000
Less your federal and state taxes at 25%	($1,250)
Less your loss of buying power with 3% inflation	($3,000)
Earnings left for you - "Net Realized Return"	$750

The interest you think you are earning is your "Gross Return" and the money left over after paying for taxes and accounting for inflation is your "Net Realized Return." In this case, expressed as a percent, your "Net Realized Return" would be less than one percent! In other words, your five percent gross interest rate would have shrunk to a net return of only .75%. That's money you'll never see again.

To be fair, history tells us that the "Gross Return" shown in the example above could be higher or lower. Interest rates change all the time. But it's also important to note that the "Gross Return" moves in response to the level of inflation. When the "Gross Return" goes up so does the cost of inflation, and consequently so do your taxes. The end result is that your "Net Realized Return" is usually about the same, not much more than zero.

Do you remember the 1970s? CD rates were over 16%! People tell me every day they wish they could earn that kind of money again on a safe investment like CDs. Wasn't that a great time? No! It wasn't. Inflation was running as high as 14%. Let's run our simple equation again with the 1970s numbers.

The interest you earn at 16% - "Gross Return"	$16,000
Less your federal and state taxes at 25%	($ 4,000)
Less your loss of buying power with 14% inflation	($14,000)
Earnings left for you - "Net Realized Return"	($ 2,000)

You would have LOST MONEY! Even with a 16 percent rate of return, the effects of taxes and inflation mean you would have lost money.

Does this "double" attack on your nest egg seem fair?
No wonder more and more people are just getting

by these days. Even folks with big nest eggs find that planning for a successful retirement can be a real challenge. Like the frog, thanks to inflation and taxes, it's easy to get into hot water and not even know it.

What ends up being deceptive to many people is that they see the value of their investments and savings accounts going up, but they haven't really factored in the loss of purchasing power caused by inflation. Plus, they may not be properly accounting for the taxes they have actually been paying on their investment earnings. The tax expense seems to get lost in the wash because it is most often paid through payroll-tax withholding, pension withholding or quarterly estimated tax-payments. To achieve your retirement dreams, you need to plan for a double attack on your buying power.

A nasty surprise…

Over the years, I've seen many people assume they're ready to retire because they've projected that their income will exceed their expenses. As an example, if your projected retirement income is $10,000 and you've budgeted for $8,000 in expenses, you might feel it's safe to retire. In reality, thanks to taxes and inflation, you could be setting yourself up for a nasty surprise ten to twenty years down the line. Why? For many people a portion of their anticipated retirement is locked in; it won't grow with inflation. Or, as in the case of Social Security income, it increases a little each year, but at a pace that is less than the inflation rate.

That's the income side; you also have to consider expenses. To start, as you move into retirement, a greater part of your budget will be allocated toward medical expenses. These costs tend to rise at a rate that is a lot faster than other expenses. So what happens? Do you remember the frog analogy I used earlier? At first everything seems fine; the water is nice and warm. You feel comfortable.

Next, other expenses grow more than you planned. Your new property tax assessment arrives; gasoline prices go up; you're hit with an unanticipated medical expense; your kids need a little extra cash to get through a tough spot...you get the picture. Your expenses go up faster than your fixed income and soon you have a real problem. What once looked like a safe and secure retirement has now turned into your worst nightmare. Your income is squeezed from both ends. Soon you find yourself being the one who writes the letter to the editor complaining that you can't afford the five-dollar increase in the garbage bill.

Retirement living is supposed to be care-free!
Now I know this scenario is simplified and exaggerated, but it highlights the potentially

devastating effects of a shrinking dollar. If you don't factor taxes and inflation into your plans for retirement, you may not reach your goals. Even folks with huge nest eggs can be forced to drastically alter their lifestyles. One of the top sources of "retirement" income today is "earned income" or wages. Many retirees are unexpectedly going back to work, selling homes they've lived in for decades or eliminating all the "fun stuff" they had planned to do in their retirements.

All of these potential pitfalls can be minimized with a little common sense planning. This is true whether you're preparing to retire in a few years or if you're already retired. In my practice, we take our clients through multiple "what-if" scenarios to pinpoint the best time to retire. Sometimes we have to readjust our thinking mid-course, but we never forget that inflation and taxes are facts of life.

Rule 4
Risk is not a four letter word!

Take calculated risks. That is quite different from being rash.
– George S. Patton

Okay, maybe "risk" does have four letters, but you don't have to wash your mouth out with soap after you say it. I think of risk like fire. Without harnessing the power and benefits of fire, you would freeze in the winter and your morning cup of coffee would taste lousy.

On the other hand, when fire is used correctly, you can stay toasty warm and curl up with a nice hot cup of cocoa next to the fireplace. Fire not respected and harnessed could spin out of control and cause untold damage. Fire used correctly can work for you. And when you plan ahead, a little fire prevention can go a long way to keeping you safe. The trick is to use fire to your advantage and protect yourself from accidents.

The same is true with risk. You need to use risk to your advantage while protecting yourself from its dangers. Some people completely avoid the use of risk and end up leading themselves down a path of slow financial disaster. Other folks throw caution to the wind and wind up with disastrous results.

How do you enjoy the benefits of risk without burning your fingers? You need to follow some basic rules for building a diversified retirement portfolio. In simpler terms, you can't put all the eggs of your nest egg in one basket. Plus, you always need to remember that time is your friend. The more you plan ahead, the easier it will be to take advantage of risk.

Would you prefer 5% or 10%?
The return on blue-chip stocks, big companies we all recognize, has averaged a little more than 10% over the past seventy years. Among other things, this period of time included World Wars, major recessions, a couple of oil crises, and years of record inflation. We live in a great country — there have been a lot of great times — but the last seven decades have had more than their fair share of terrible events. Yet, through thick and thin, well-managed portfolios of blue-chip stocks have created tremendous wealth for people from all walks of life. But they have only worked for those who have been willing to take on some risk.

Do you think there are plenty of things to worry about today? Do you worry about the threat of terrorism? But to put things in perspective, don't you think those who were living in the 1940s were worried about the Japanese? We worried about the Russians in the 1970s. Have you built your bomb shelter yet? Is the unemployment rate a worry? What about for the people in the Great Depression of the 1930s?

Are gas prices too high today? Think back to the Carter Administration and gas rationing in the 1970s. Today we complain about corporate greed and lament the Enron scandal, but think about early industry in the U.S. and the sweat shops. We say society's morals are declining. Have you ever read the Old Testament or considered the love-ins from the 1960s?

There is always something to worry about! We have always had and will always have real worries and real concerns. But through all the years, a well-managed portfolio that uses time-tested disciplines has made money for patient investors.

On the flip side, fixed income investments like bonds and CDs, which are generally viewed as "safe" investments, have averaged about five percent. Over the same seventy years, the return on these seemingly conservative investments has been less than half of the return on blue-chip stocks. In my mind, investing in bonds and CDs is like riding a stationary bike; there is a lot of activity going on but you're not getting anywhere. Remember, taxes and inflation eat away the majority of returns when you're only earning five percent.

Is it worth trying to earn 10% instead of 5%? Let's look at a simplified answer to this question. The following table shows the value of $100,000 invested over different time frames at both rates of return.

	5 percent	10 percent
1 year	$105,000	$110,000
3 years	$115,763	$133,000
5 years	$127,628	$161,051
10 years	$162,889	$259,374

In each time period, putting risk aside, the benefit of earning 10% increases. Over 10 years, when using the 5 percent approach you end up with $62,889 in earnings while the 10 percent approach gives you $159,374. Doubling your return means you would more than double the dollars you could put in your pocket. In this case, it's a difference of $96,845 - just shy of $100,000. Coincidentally, the difference alone represents about the amount we started with in the example.

The above table is only true if you actually average these two different rates of return; it is an overly-simplified example. Unfortunately, life is rarely average, so planning for averages can be dangerous. This is where understanding that four-letter word "risk" comes into play.

Fathers know best

We are all wired differently. Risk can mean different things to different people. Risk can affect different people in different ways. While I was growing up, my father owned a small construction company. He told me he would never criticize one of his workers for being afraid to do a task; he simply expected hard work. One of my father's best employees was afraid of heights, so he never asked him to climb tall ladders. My father instinctively understood something important about human behavior. Emotions almost always override logic. Instead of trying to force an issue, it can be better to find another way to accomplish a job.

The same can be said about investment risk. You need to understand your limitations and find ways to work around them in your long-term retirement plans. As an advisor, my job is to find constructive ways to help my clients accomplish their goals within the boundaries of their concerns about risk. Forcing the risk issue is a sure way to cause hard feelings and lose a lot of sleep.

How does risk make you feel?

I can recall an incident with one of my clients in which I probably did a poor job of understanding their acceptance of risk. During the first couple months I managed this couple's portfolio, they saw it grow from $500,000 to $525,000. When they got their monthly statements, they called to share their excitement. Of course, this doesn't always happen; it was just a good 60 days for the stock market.

Regrettably, the account value went down to $515,000 in the third month. The stock market, as it often does, took back some of the profits this couple had seen when they reviewed their monthly statements. Again they called me, but this time they were in a panic because they felt like they had lost money. Even though they understood that their portfolio had increased from $500,000 to $515,000 over three months, the drop from the $525,000 level in the prior month was more than they could handle.

An improper risk assessment caused these clients to lose sleep. The $10,000 drop in market value in the third month was more worrisome than the $15,000 increase over the entire 90-day period of time. It didn't matter whose mistake it was, we quickly fixed the problem by reducing their risk exposure. It's always better to adjust the risk profile of a portfolio down a notch or two than to suffer through years of worry and doubt.

If any course of action is going to make you sit straight up in bed at night with a panic attack, you shouldn't do it. I have experienced events in my own life that have caused me to break out into a cold sweat for several days at a time. Believe me, it just isn't worth it. A successful retirement should be filled with many nights of peaceful sleep.

Fear, stupidity and greed
Too many people look only at what could go wrong-they overstate the negative, and never really look at the potential payoff. I hear statements like, "I can lose all my money in the stock market." Now let me ask you a question, "Can you show a time in all of modern history where a major stock market went to zero?" The Great Depression, the crash of 1987 and the years from 2000 through 2002 are all examples of terrible times for stocks. But the market did not go to zero; it has always come back stronger than before.

Sure, some people lose money they can't afford to lose during bad markets, but in most cases they're doing stupid things. The desire to get rich quick can be overwhelming. I've seen folks throw caution to the wind and borrow money to invest when they don't have the resources to repay their debts. Other investors get caught up in the exuberance of the good times and simply forget the importance of diversifying their retirement nest eggs. Still other seemingly-sane investors squander large sums of money with excessive day trading. It's horrifying to watch otherwise intelligent people approach investing their life's savings like a trip to Las Vegas.

A reality check

Remember, the market has never gone to zero. In fact, most everyone makes money in stocks if they commit to at least a five-year holding period. Even investors who purchased stocks at the market peak in 2000 made it all back by the year 2006. That's a long time to wait for a recovery, but it's also the worst example I can give you in the last 50 years. We need to give stocks the respect they deserve and, like fire, harness their staggering potential power to work in our best interest.

Think about it this way. On average, the stock market loses money once every four years. This means there is about a one in four chance you'll see your portfolio decline in any given twelve-month period of time. It's also possible that two or three of these down years could come one right after the other; your portfolio could lose value for two or three consecutive years. This is reality! So if you need to buy a car in the next year or two, I wouldn't advise you to invest those funds in the stock market. There's a one in four chance you'll be riding a bicycle instead.

On the other hand, if you're willing to give your stock investments at least five years, your odds improve dramatically. One out of seven times you could lose, but six out of seven times you'll make money. If your investment horizon is at least ten years, you have an almost 100% chance of making money.

But, I don't have 10 years...

Now, here's where a lot of smart folks may make a big mistake. As they approach retirement they decide that they don't have the five or ten years it takes to invest in stocks. They're concerned by the fact that they're no longer saving, and will need to use their investments for income. They decide stocks no longer have a place in their portfolios. Given the realties of investing in stocks we covered above, this seems logical.

But the average 65-year-old will spend more than twenty years, perhaps even thirty or forty years, in retirement. If they structure their portfolios the right way, they do have time for stocks to work. Besides, in their early retirement years, most retirees will avoid spending their principal; they're going to be spending the income their principal generates. And, even if they are going to be spending their principal, they will most likely be spending only a small portion of it. Hopefully, the bulk of their money will be invested for ten years or longer.

Slicing the pie

A successful retirement often means breaking your money down into several different investment categories. It's like cutting a pie into slices; the size of the pieces may vary based on your appetite at the time you eat it. One category for your retirement nest egg might be the money you'll need for your living expenses over the next two years. You could place these assets in short-term investments like money market funds or CDs. A second category could cover the next eight or so year time segment and be invested in bonds that will mature in three to ten years. Finally, the third category could be the investments you'll hold for longer than ten years, giving you an opportunity to invest in stocks.

Retirement is a time to be more conservative. You're not adding to your nest egg, so it can be more difficult to recover from financial setbacks. But the fact remains that over longer periods of time you should make more money in stocks than you would in bonds or CDs. Striking the right balance is the key to adjusting your risk for a long and rewarding retirement.

Rule 5
Diversify and look for the best of the best!

Divide your portion to seven or even eight, for you do not know what misfortune may occur on the earth.
- Ecclesiastes 11:12

It's not one thing we do 100% better than anyone else, but 100 things we do 1% better than everyone else.
- London O's Game Programme

Think of your retirement nest egg like making pies for a church bake sale. You've been asked to do all the baking because you make the best pies. The pressure is on because this event will be the only fundraiser your church holds all year. You can't afford a flop!

You know it would be easier to make one type of pie than a bunch of different types, but you don't know what people will be hungry for on the day of the sale. At the last church picnic, a lot of folks loved your apple pie, but you know some people prefer pumpkin pie. As you look through your recipe box, you realize that over the years you've made pecan (my personal favorite), cherry, peach and banana cream pies for church events. And you've never come home with leftovers!

What should you make?
Apple pies are the easiest to make, but if you make them and everyone wants pumpkin pie the day of the bake sale, you've struck out. You may cut back on your work and make a few bucks, but nothing like you're expecting. You'll be devastated and the church won't have the money it was counting on.

If you guess right and make pumpkin pies, you'll make a ton of money for the church. Pumpkin pies are more work, but it would've been worth the extra effort. But can you really take this chance? Remember, this is the biggest fundraiser of the year. Is this the right time to swing for the fences?

If you make half of your pies apple and the other half pumpkin, you'll be hedging your bets. It will also take a good deal of extra work and planning. Making one pie is always easier. You know you won't hit a homerun, but you should make a nice profit. Plus, you've taken some of the risk out of the equation.

If you get ambitious and do some really good planning, you could make all of your favorite pies – apple, pumpkin, cherry, pecan (my personal favorite), peach, and banana cream. You'll increase your odds of making more people happy. Sales should be stronger. And you won't have to take the chance of guessing on just one pie. The extra work and planning will be worth the effort.

Is your mouth watering for pie?
Now that I've whetted your appetite for some homemade pie, let's get back to your retirement nest egg. You have several different options for deciding on the right investments. Each option carries different risks and rewards. Some require little work and effort, while others require more planning. The only thing your options have in common is that they're providing income for your one and only retirement.

You can't afford to flop!

You could certainly leave your money invested in the apple pie. In other words, keep doing things the way you've always done them. After all, you've done okay and it's comfortable. Plus, it requires a lot less effort and planning.

On the other hand, you could look for the one great investment that will make you a fortune – the pumpkin pie. It will take a little more work up front, but once you've made your decision you'll be on easy street. Or will you constantly be looking over your shoulder wondering if you made the right decision? Can you really afford to take this chance with your life's savings?

Some planning is better than no planning. And you've always liked to hedge your bets, so you could put half of your money in something with more risk and play it safe with the rest. You guessed it – pumpkin pies and apple pies. It's better than just maintaining status quo and you're not swinging for the fences. It could be a good compromise, but do you really want to compromise with your retirement?

Finally, you could plan for a lot of different pies – apple, pumpkin, cherry, pecan (again, my personal favorite), peach, and banana cream. You'll be diversified. You won't have your retirement nest egg in one basket. This extra effort will increase your odds of success. Reaching outside your comfort zone will give you more options for an enjoyable retirement. And you won't have to take the chance of guessing on just one pie.

No one really knows which kind of pie is going to sell the best at the bake sale, so we hedge our bet. And yes, there is some mathematical science behind how these selections are made, but that's too boring to go into now. Besides, I need a slice of pecan pie!

Are you ready for a pie shop?
Now that you've mastered the church bake sale, it's time to open a pie shop. In doing your research, you find some historical information as to which pies have sold the best in the past. But this is a totally new year and customers' tastes may have changed some. You hope that each pie you decide to make does sell, and sells at a great price, but it probably won't.

There is always going to be one pie that you end up selling at a discount. And there will be another pie that flies off the racks and sells at a premium. You won't really know which one until you make your first pies and open your shop. Once you see how your pies sell, you may change your line up- making more of the ones that sell the best, making fewer of the decent sellers, eliminating those that don't sell at all and adding new ones as time permits.

Investments are just like pies in pie shops; they come in different flavors. They need to be placed in portfolios in differing amounts. They won't all perform well at the same time, but in combination they should produce consistent results over time.

When I go out and search for pie makers to help stock my clients' pie shops, I look for the best of the best. A lot of people make banana cream pies, but only a select few make the tastiest. Others are great at pecan pies, but may make lousy apple pies. So I go somewhere else to find my apple pies. I want to find pie makers who put all their energy into being the best at their specialty. There's no reason to settle for second best.

Turning pies into assets classes
In the world of investments, the pies in the pie shop are asset classes. Instead of flavors, we call them things like stocks, bonds and cash. Each of these major categories can be broken down into smaller groups, just like there are different types of apple pie.

Stocks can be split up into categories like value, growth and international, which can further be divided by size - small, medium and large. Bonds can be split up by maturity - short, medium and long term. They can also be divided by quality; you may be familiar with terms like investment grade bonds and junk bonds. Cash could be savings accounts, money market funds or treasury bills.

One way to simplify matters is to use mutual funds. Mutual funds by themselves are not an asset class, but they are placed into groups based on the way they invest. For example, in industry jargon, you could have a "small cap international fund" – a stock fund that invests in small companies that are located around the world. As an investment manager, I can then look for the best fund in this category if I believe my clients should have this type of pie (or asset class) in their portfolios.

Keep in mind there are over 10,000 mutual funds, so picking the right ones isn't always as easy as it might sound. That's why it makes sense for most folks to use a financial advisor. Good advisors do a lot of homework. They pick the best funds, select the right combinations and monitor them closely to watch for surprises.

Do your funds have a family?
I run into a lot of retirees who are invested in just one family of mutual funds. In other words, they work with a company that has a bunch of different funds that invest in several asset classes. This is not disastrous, but most fund families don't have top performers in all categories. So these investors may be getting the best performance in one asset class, but only mediocre performance in another.

In my practice, we like to mix and match different fund families in our clients' portfolios. It goes back to what I mentioned earlier about selecting the best pie makers. You need to work with the best of the best. It's a little subjective (even the best funds have bad years), but the work and planning that goes into selecting the right funds is well worth the effort.

If you have a broker who uses a commission-based approach to managing your portfolio (often called "load" funds), he is almost ethically required to use just one family of funds. That's because you are entitled to a lower commission based on the amount of money you put into each fund family. If it's an ethical broker using a good family of funds, you could be okay. But the limitation to one fund family may work against you. You won't be invested in the best of the best.

Similar problems can occur for do-it-yourself investors who use "no load" fund families. I also see a lot with folks who have large company-sponsored retirement accounts, like 401(k)s, who only use a single fund family. These fund families may be cheap, convenient or, in the case of retirement plans, required, but they don't always give you the best of the best.

High returns aren't everything.
A lot of folks come to see me with portfolios filled with the top-performing funds they've read about in financial magazines. They've made their investment choices based solely on the returns. They're mesmerized by reports of a 50% return in three short months. After all, it seems logical to assume that a fund that did well last year, or over the last three years, will continue to break the bank. Unfortunately, past performance is not a great predictor of future results. I've seen cases where it would have been better to pick a fund

that had a lousy year than one that had a good year. Over time, choosing the right asset allocation for your portfolio of funds is much more important than chasing returns.

One other thing usually happens when you chase performance; you end up with funds that are like clones of each other. Funds in specific asset classes tend to perform similarly. If you buy last year's best performers, you may buy five different funds that invest in the same things. You're not really buying five different flavors of pie. You're buying the same flavor from five different pie shops.

Never take your eye off the ball.
I want my clients to own the best of the best and hold for the long term, but over time some funds will change in quality. Management and policies change at mutual fund companies all the time. Sometimes egos and greed get in the way of common sense. My goal with my clients is to "buy-and-hold," *not to* "buy-and-forget."

Mutual fund managers should be reviewed on a regular basis to make sure they are still the best of the best. One of the tools I use to pick funds ranks them on a one to five star basis. If one of my managers starts out with five-star rating and falls to four stars, I'm probably going to hang onto them. It's tough to stay on the very top, so some funds may move back and forth between the top two ratings. On the other hand, if the manager drops to a three-star rating, I almost always look for a replacement.

Plan ahead, diversify, be choosy and monitor frequently.
I've covered a lot of ground in this chapter because I've seen a lot of people ruin their retirements by making simple investment mistakes.

• It's easy to be complacent and not plan ahead.
• Everybody understands diversification, but not everybody does it properly.
• Picking a mutual fund with a good track record is as easy as reading the latest financial magazines, but it may not be the right fund for your portfolio.
• Whether you're planning or living in retirement, it's easy to get comfortable and forget to monitor your nest egg.

Whether you work with a professional or not, you need to take your investment planning seriously. The simplest mistakes can have a lifelong impact. The wrong move at the wrong time could make the difference between enjoying your retirement and going back to work to make more pies.

Rule 6

Do you really need bonds and CDs?

The race is not always to the swift, nor the battle to the strong, but that's the way to bet.
– Damon Runyon

We've covered the potentially-devastating impact of taxes and inflation on fixed income investments like bonds. You understand that not all risk is bad, so stocks sound like a good place for your retirement nest egg. This may lead you to wonder, "Why do people buy bonds?" Frankly, some people have a ton of money. They can support their income needs without leaning on the superior returns of stocks. In other words, they don't have to take any risk.

If you're in this category – congratulations! But please make sure you run your numbers properly. To live a successful retirement, you can't afford a mathematical error. It would be like planning a flight to the moon and forgetting to fill your fuel tank. Remember, as we discussed under the section on taxes and inflation, some people are sadly mistaken by the income potential of their investments. They wind up in a fixed income squeeze.

Bonds are like sleeping pills.
In reality, most of us don't have the luxury that the income from our safe investments will cover all of our future needs and desires. Bonds, CDs, money market funds and savings accounts won't generate the same levels of returns as a well-managed portfolio of stocks. We need to accept some risk and seek higher returns in stocks.

This doesn't mean you need to take bonds or other safe investments off the table. The returns may be lower, but they can also add stability to your portfolio. If you can't sleep at night knowing you have all of your money in stocks, bonds can give you some peace of mind. Bonds are like sleeping pills. When used in the right doses, sleeping pills may be good for your health. Similarly, the right mix of bonds can keep you from making bad decisions when times get tough.

A power boat race...
Consider another analogy. You're preparing for a power boat race. You'll be speeding across a long lake on a very windy day. It's going to be rough

and your boat is going to take a pounding. Your objective will be to get from one end of the lake to the other as quickly as possible. You realize that you stand a good chance of cracking your hull if your boat bounces too much in the windy waves.

You also know that if you have to completely stop your boat to patch a leak you'll almost certainly lose. So you consider throwing a few rocks in the bottom of the boat for protection against the choppy waters. You believe stability may be more important than raw speed. The rocks will slow you down a bit, but you won't have to stop for repairs.

Using bonds is like throwing a few rocks in the bottom of your boat. Sure they may limit your returns, but their stability could keep you on track. You won't be worried about having too much money in stocks. You won't abandon your game plan in the middle of your retirement. You'll achieve your goals and be able to sleep at night along the way.

Rule 7
Zero debt is the best.

Credit buying is much like being drunk; the buzz happens immediately, and it gives you a lift. The hangover comes the day after.
- Dr. Joyce Brothers

Debt is the slavery of the free.
- Publilius Syrus

I think a successful retirement is a debt-free retirement. There is no need for car loans or credit card debt. I push my clients to set a goal of having their retirement home paid off by the time they retire. I've watched a lot of retirees over the years; the ones who are the most content are those who have their houses paid off. With your house paid off, you will simply need less cash to live on. If you have a $1,000 monthly mortgage payment, you need about $250,000 in investments to generate enough income to make your payments. That's a lot of money.

Is your house an investment?

The basis for most of my concepts around debt is that I view your house as a consumption item - like a car. Most people think of their houses as an investment. To me, once you've purchased your house; you've spent the money. It then becomes a question of how and when you plan to pay for it.

You might get a warm fuzzy feeling watching your house value go up, but let's think about this for a moment. If you plan to step up to a bigger or better house someday, the cost of that house is probably increasing in value as well (If you don't believe me, just go back and read the chapter on inflation). So yes, you will get more dollars out of selling your house, but the new one will cost just that much more. You are not really getting ahead.

People sometimes think they'll step down to a smaller house when they retire. This way they'll be able to get their profits out of the house they sell. In my experience, this rarely happens. The older we get, the more comfortable we become with our homes. Many of the folks who actually buy smaller homes simultaneously step up the quality and/or improve their location, so they don't pocket much profit.

For planning purposes, I think it's better to just face the music. You spent the money and now you're going to be paying a ton of interest. Not that this is totally a bad thing; you have to live somewhere. Plus, if you didn't own a home you would be paying rent. And you get some tax breaks.

Overall, I believe home ownership is something we all need to experience. My only concern is the mental games we play with ourselves. It's easy to fall prey to all the high-pressure real estate and mortgage marketing. Too many folks buy too much house, and they buy it before they can really afford it. They would be better off starting small and paying for their house more quickly. Sure, this might mean they miss some quality of living and house appreciation, but it's more than offset by avoiding a ton in interest.

I practice what I preach.
Over the years, I've watched many young people buy huge houses. They mistakenly believe they need the tax write-off, so they don't worry about having a big mortgage. Listen, I'm a CPA (I even have a master's in taxation); I know a thing or two about taxes. My home is paid off. In fact, I've never had a home loan for more than six years.

You can pay for a house more than three times over when you pay all that mortgage interest. I only wanted to pay for my house once, so I started out modestly. The first one, back in 1988, cost only $42,000. I lived on the second floor and the first floor was my tax office. I paid for this house in four years, even though my income was only around $40,000 during this time period.

When I met my wife, she had just bought a house. We paid for it in six years. Next, we saved hard, the stock market did well and I made a good real estate investment. This allowed us to purchase our dream home with cash. We still live in this ranch home on ten acres.

What logic did I go through to convince myself to have no home loans? I'll admit interest rates were a little higher back then, but that wasn't the only reason. I wanted to limit my risk. If I paid off my house, I'm guaranteed that I don't have to make a house payment next month. The only way I could earn more money than I would be paying in interest is if I invested in the stock market. I may have won out, but it wouldn't be guaranteed; the security of having a fully-paid-for home was much more important.

It all comes down to risk.
If I pay off my home, I'm guaranteed that I don't have to make a house payment next month. That's a great feeling. But investing in the stock market to earn more than my mortgage payments means I'm taking on some risk. Some months I'll earn more than my payments and some months I'll earn less. There's no way to know for sure where I'll end up.

When evaluating risk I like to compare apples to apples, so looking at the 10% average return of the stock market is not even the best comparison.

A mortgage interest rate is more like a bond, CD or other fixed income investment. If you look around for good quality fixed income investments, the best rates are usually about the same as prevailing mortgage rates. In other words, you're paying about the same as you're earning. You're not really getting that far ahead.

Actually, now that my house is paid off, I have a solid foundation fortifying my net worth. I can afford to take more risk, so my initial avoidance of risk might actually help me make more money in other ways. As I said earlier in this book, risk can be a good thing. But it can only work for you if you have staying power, which is the ability to hang in there through the tough times.

What about the taxes I save with my mortgage payments?

If you have the money to pay off your mortgage, but instead keep it invested, you'll still have to pay taxes on the interest, dividends and gains you earn. All the mortgage interest does is offset some of your investment earnings. It's usually a pretty even swap. You don't get as much bang for the buck out of your mortgage deduction as you think you do.

If you want to know how much your mortgage deduction really saves you, run a couple of sample tax returns. Keep your mortgage deduction and investment earnings in the first return and eliminate them in the second return. You might find that your standard deduction will give you back the bulk of the mortgage deduction you think you are losing. For most people, the tax savings is about one or two months of payments. Uncle Sam gets two house payments and you keep ten. Is it really worth it? Or would you feel more comfortable knowing you don't have a mortgage payment at all?

Okay, forget the numbers...
It's easy to talk numbers when you consider the benefits of having a mortgage, but there's more to life than taxes and investments. Paying off my mortgage was a blessing. First, it allowed my wife to retire and stay home with our kids. How do you put a dollar value on that?

At the time we paid off our mortgage, we had one child. No mortgage meant we could adopt two additional children out of an orphanage in South Korea. Once again, it's hard to quantify the value of this on their lives and ours. Our decision has given us huge peace of mind and a lot of personal freedom.

On the financial side, I started putting about half of the amount that would have gone to a house payment into a separate investment account (I have used the other half to pre-pay for college for the kids and save for cars). After only six years without a mortgage, this fund is approaching six figures. By the time I retire, it could completely support me and my wife. If this is the only financial thing I do right in my own life, my retirement will be secure, my wife will have been able to stay home with our kids and we will have been a big help to two orphan children. That's awesome.

Another blessing I was able to receive by having my house paid off was helping my mother. One of my core values is taking care of my extended family. Mom's only retirement income was Social Security. She was still working a part-time job when she should have been retired. Mom never owned a house. She tried to rent nice apartments, but she could only afford run-down places.

Using a government program for first-time home buyers, I was able to move her into a brand spanking new, although very modest, house. The money I put down was under $1,000 and the payment was less than some people pay for their cars, but I bought Mom a house! I could afford the payment because I didn't have any debt. I fulfilled one of my lifetime dreams. And my mom had quality housing and a rent payment, zero, which would never go up.

So, you want to take some risk???
I just finished reading a fancy advertisement trying to convince people that the money they have sitting in their home equity is earning 0% - it's

dead money. It's not dead money, it's preventing me from making a house payment, and it's avoiding interest expense. They are only looking at one side of the equation.

What the advertisers want in this situation is for you to borrow on your house and pay them interest. Plus, they want you to invest that money into something that will pay them a commission. They are taking your money two ways. Stay smart; don't let them rip you off.

This latest angle is called equity harvesting. You borrow money on your house and invest it somewhere. But if you invest the money the way these hucksters suggest, into a life insurance policy, you lose your mortgage deduction. It just doesn't make any sense. It's a losing strategy.

Is it ever a good strategy to borrow against your home?
There are times when you should not pay off your home. Each situation is different and needs to be carefully reviewed. For some folks, paying off their mortgage would mean using up too much of their emergency money. You always need to protect your backside so you don't end up in a financial corner. If you're retired and have a sizable home loan, it's sometimes unrealistic to find ways to pay it off. You need to implement a strategy that maximizes your cash flow instead of one that maximizes your net worth.

There are also some people who don't have enough cash flow from their investments, Social Security and pensions to cover their expenses. If you don't have adequate cash flow, you might need to use the equity in your home to create more investment income with the hope that you can earn more than the loan will cost. Be careful with this approach; you're increasing your risk profile.

As much as I encourage people to have their homes free in clear; I'm not against appropriate levels of debt in solid business endeavors or real estate investments. As long as the money is going to something that is making money, producing positive cash flow or going up in value, it may make sense. Wise business managers with experience know how to take money and put it to work to make more money. They know how to keep debt to manageable levels.

Go for zero debt.
I think a successful retirement is a debt-free retirement. You can take a lot of the stress and risk out of the best years of your life. You deserve it!

Rule 8

Experience, ethics and education make a difference when it comes to picking your retirement planning advisors!

Life is a succession of lessons, which must be lived to be understood.
- Ralph Waldo Emerson

Never trust the advice of a man in difficulties.
- Aesop

Whether you're planning for retirement or already living successfully in retirement, you need to be sure you have excellent support. Whether you work with a single advisor or group of specialists, experience can make a huge difference. Work with professionals who take the time and money to continuously invest in their businesses and education.

Let me toot my own horn.
After completing my four-year degree, I went to work for a huge international accounting firm. Having grown up on a farm, I quickly determined that a big company was not a good fit. I enjoyed accounting, so I went back to school to gain a master's degree in Taxation. Then I started my own Certified Public Accounting (CPA) firm when I was just 26 years old.

I worked hard, brought in a lot of great clients, hired some terrific teammates and taught myself how to run a successful business. It was a challenging time, but it was also a lot of fun. Along the way, I even helped a few other folks grow their businesses and sell them for nice profits.

Being a lifelong learner and a bit of a bookworm, I decided to become a Certified Financial Planner (CFP) too. I figured that even if I didn't add financial planning to the list of services I offered my clients, it would still help me become a better accountant. This took three years, with an average study time of about 20 hours per week, all while I was running my CPA practice.

Now, just to maintain both my CPA and CFP designations, I take between 40 and 60 hours of technical training each year. This continuing education is in addition to the multiple newsletters and magazines I read every month. The world is constantly changing, and keeping up with the latest knowledge is critical. Plus, I am very serious about what I do for my clients and I want to be among the best in my profession.

Blah, blah, blah...
That's enough about me. But I want to be sure you understand why I went into such detail. Choosing an advisor or a team of advisors to help you achieve a successful retirement is not easy. Whether you work with one person or multiple people, you need to look for a combination of experience, ethics and education.

In addition to the obvious need for investment, tax and financial planning expertise, your advisory team may need to include some other professionals. Sometimes all of these folks will work together in a single firm, but more often than not your primary advisor will need to coordinate with a group of outside specialists. You may pick some of these specialists yourself or your advisor may refer you to the folks he trusts the most.

Don't be fooled by impressive sounding credentials.
There are a lot of impressive sounding credentials

for financial advisors these days. In fact, there seems to be a new one everyday. Some can be earned in just a few days. For some, you can just write a check. You need to watch out for advisors who may be overstating their credentials.

For example, words like Certified Senior Advisor may sound good, but you need to be cautious. The title obviously has an impressive tone, but what was done to earn this designation? Many of these three-word titles are just marketing gimmicks. Quite often, individuals using these newer credentials are strictly selling annuities to senior citizens. I have even seen them put on a seminar and feed you a nice steak dinner to get you to come and listen to them. I would prefer that you choose your financial advisor by asking someone you trust for a referral, not based on whether your steak was cooked properly.

If you are looking for qualified financial advice, look for a "Certified Financial Planner" (CFP) or a "Certified Public Accountant" (CPA) who specializes in financial planning. Look for someone with a "JD," a law degree, who specializes in estate planning. Other important qualifications for those from the insurance industry include individuals with the ChFC, "Chartered Financial Consultant," or CLU, "Chartered Life Underwriter."

The point I'm trying to make is that there are fields of study that have taken years of hard work and discipline to achieve. At the same time, there are designations that can be obtained by attending a weekend seminar and writing a check. The easy to obtain certifications sound as impressive as the real deal; you need to be wary of the pretenders.

Work with someone who has actually created wealth before.
Let me ask you an important question.
If your minister just went through an ugly divorce, would you want him to give your son and his fiancée marriage counseling? If your mechanic couldn't make it into the shop because his car broke down, would you want him to work on your car?

There are a lot of advisors giving advice who don't have their own financial plan; they haven't created wealth for themselves. I realize this may sound like the chicken or the egg problem. In other words, you can't get experience without experimenting on some clients and you can't get clients without some experience. But do you really want to be someone's guinea pig?

In the financial planning world, people can be trained for 30 days and then they are turned loose on the public to sell something. I call them "30-day wonder." They can be dangerous. Forget these folks and find an advisor who has actually been successful with their own money and with their clients' money.

Maybe it's politically incorrect to ask some of the questions you really want to know. It's probably impolite to ask someone how much money they make or ask to look at their net worth statement, but isn't this exactly the knowledge you need to know? Don't you want to know if this person has been successful with his own money and not just someone who bought a nice suit on his credit card?

The next best thing would be to learn to ask important questions of the individual you're interviewing to manage your money. The Certified Financial Planning Board suggests you ask these questions:

1. What experience do you have (retirement, investment, tax, estate, insurance, comprehensive planning)?
2. What are your qualifications? What designations or certifications do you have? What are your areas of specialization?
3. What services do you offer?
4. How long have you been offering financial planning advice to clients? Please describe your work history.
5. What are your educational qualifications? How many hours of new training do you undertake each year?
6. What is your approach to financial planning?
7. Will you be the only person working with me?
8. How will I pay for your services?

9. How much do you typically charge?
10. Could anyone besides me benefit from your recommendations? In other words, do you have any conflicts of interest? Is any of your compensation based on selling products? Do you pay anyone a referral fee for sending business to you? Do you have a business affiliation with any company whose products or services you are recommending?
11. Have you ever been publicly disciplined for any unlawful or unethical actions in your professional career?
12. Will you put all your answers and your services in writing?

Work with a good attorney.
Successfully planning your retirement means you need to have a solid plan for passing your nest egg on to your heirs. Work with an attorney who thoroughly understands estate planning. There are lots of different types of lawyers and many specialties. Don't just assume that the attorney who helped you close on your last house purchase understands the latest trends in retirement planning. Don't settle for a generalist. You might pay a little more, but it's like the old Fran Oil Filter commercials – "Pay me now or pay me later." And paying later can be much more expensive.

Even though I preach the need for having a good attorney, it's also worth mentioning that attorneys are generally not the best point people for your retirement planning needs. The time and effort that goes into being a good lawyer makes it difficult to keep up with investment management and financial planning strategies. Your attorney should be willing to accept the role that best fits his ability to help you achieve your goals.

Work with a good insurance agent.
A good insurance agent understands the proper amounts and the proper types of insurance for retirees. This is true whether you're talking about car insurance or life insurance. Most good agents are ethical and will work within the plan your primary advisor has created. They're willing to be part of a team that will help you live successfully in retirement.

Stay away from agents who profess to be one-stop retirement planning specialists, but don't have the necessary experience. Many insurance salespeople have a limited number of tools in their toolbox. If all you have is a hammer, sooner or later everything starts to look like a nail. If you ever went to an insurance agent for "free financial planning," is it any wonder that the eventual recommendation somehow involved a lot of life insurance?

The many different types of insurance are just components of a complete financial plan; they needs to be used properly. You need to have adequate coverage, but you don't need to overdo it. Work with an agent who understands the need to be part of your retirement planning team.

Special note: Later in this book I'll review three primary areas of insurance that are of concern to retirees – long-term care, life insurance and annuities.

It's your team!
As someone who is planning for retirement or is already retired, you're like the owner of a sports team. Whether you work with a single advisor who acts as your point person or with a group of specialists, the professionals who oversee your plan are your players; each one plays a special role on your team. They all need to work together with and be committed to your long-term retirement success.

68

Rule 9

How should you pay for advice?

Be wary of the man who urges an action in which he himself incurs no risk.
- Joaquin Setanti

Others will follow your footsteps easier than they will your advice.
– Unknown

One of the most difficult parts of selecting advisors to help you plan and enjoy a successful retirement is deciding the best way to pay for advice. With bankers, brokers, accountants, money managers and insurance people all wanting you to use their services, you have a lot of options.

But don't get carried away. How you pay for advice is not nearly as important as finding an advisor you can trust. Once you find an advisor you can trust, you need to clearly understand how the advisor is paid. You should be comfortable that you are receiving good value for your money.

Nobody works for free...
You would never take a job if you weren't going to be paid, so you shouldn't look for an advisor who'll work for nothing. You probably won't find one. Sure, there are some advisors who say their services are free or that their fees are the cheapest, but you have to view them with a little suspicion. Quality advice is rarely free and it almost never comes from the lowest cost provider.

In the world of financial advice, everyone gets paid. You just need to know how. As with any major purchase, you need to be an informed consumer. The trick is to do enough homework to be sure you understand how an advisor is paid for their service and advice. If the price is reasonable and you have confidence in their integrity, you're ready to move forward.

Should I pay upfront commissions?
Many investment products, annuity policies and insurance contracts are riddled with hidden fees and costs. Commissions are typically paid up front to the advisor who sells the product. The commission either comes directly out of the money you invest or from increased annual expenses, and there may be a penalty if you sell the investment too quickly.

Commissions aren't necessarily bad as long as you know what you are paying and feel it's fair. The biggest complaint I have about commission-based advisors is that they tend to be too focused on a one-time sale. They forget about ongoing service after the sale. Have you ever purchased a life insurance policy or made an investment in a portfolio of mutual funds? After the sale, were you promised annual check-ups? I hate to say it, but it probably didn't happen or at least not consistently over time. That's all too common in the financial services business today.

My own current insurance company for home, auto and umbrella liability policies skipped any kind of review for the first five years. Recently they began sending letters stating it was time for my annual review. Unfortunately the agent who was there when I first signed up had retired and I had a new person. He was a nice enough guy but the checkup was cursory at best and he moved right into his real purpose and that was to sell me additional life and long-term care insurance.

Here's what I hear over and over when I meet with potential new clients for the first time. They tell me their advisors were very interested in visiting with them when they had a bunch of money to invest. The advisors were eager; they called all the time and had fancy brochures and glorious projections. As consumers, they knew they were paying upfront commissions for the products they were buying, but they felt the cost was reasonable.

After the initial sale was over, they quickly uncovered a big mistake. They assumed the commission and all the sales hype included ongoing service. It turns out their advisors were only interested in the big sale; their service promises were full of hot air. The client may or may not have a good investment, but they know they don't have a trusted advisor.

If you're unsure if you'll be paying a commission or not, just ask your advisor how much money you'll get back if you change your mind one day after you make an initial investment. If you won't get it all back, you'll most likely have paid a commission (This excludes the "free look" period offered some life insurance and annuity products).

A typical commission is around five percent up front. But I've even seen cases when the amount is over ten percent. I have a client who came to me 60 days after he invested $200,000 in an insurance policy. He had changed his mind and was looking for a something better. Unfortunately, he would lose $40,000 to back-end commissions if he liquidated. Commissions aren't necessarily bad, but you need to understand what and how you're paying for advice.

I once had a Series 7 broker's licensee to be able to sell mutual funds and other investment products. I was a fully-licensed broker. I also had an insurance license and was set up to sell life insurance and annuities. Both approaches paid me through commissions. I surrendered these licenses because something inside me just didn't feel right. Not that it was wrong in itself; it just wasn't my style. As a consumer, you may feel the same way.

What about ongoing fees?
As an investment advisor, I work on a fee-only basis. This means I don't take a commission. I do get paid for my services, but it's a gradual payment. I earn an agreed upon percentage of the investments I manage. My fee is a lot less than most upfront commission charges. My services for investment management work and financial planning range from .05% to 1.33% per year depending on the size of your account. If you average all my clients together it comes out to 0.08%; that's less than 1%!

I feel this way of charging for services puts me on the same side of the table as my clients because the better I do, the more I will be paid. If my clients make less money, I will make less money. My clients can also take their money somewhere else without taking a big commission hit. Plus, it keeps me in front of my clients. I have to regularly hold individual client reviews to talk about my results. My clients stay well informed.

As an over-simplified example, if you had $100,000 to invest with a broker and the commission you paid was five percent, you would have paid $5,000 to have someone invest and watch your money. Now, most advisors are ethical people and they intend to give you ongoing service. But it's only human nature that after they have your money invested, they become more interested in obtaining more new clients. They want to find another $5,000 commission and have less time to give you good service.

To continue the example, if you invested the same $100,000 with a fee-only advisor, you would be charged around 1 1/3% in first year fees – about $1,350. This payment is generally spread out evenly throughout the year. This significantly reduces your upfront charges and decreases your risk. If your advisor wants to keep earning this fee, he'll have to do a good job of managing your money and providing ongoing service.

In addition to avoiding spending the $5,000 on commission you will earn investment income on this amount. This further reduces your effective out-of-pocket cost. I also continuously look to invest your money into the lowest cost investments possible, probably saving you even more.

I designed my business to keep my clients' out-of-pocket expenses low because this helps my clients make more money over time. If my clients make money they will stay with me and send me referrals to more potential clients. It's a win-win for me and my clients.

The Golden Rule

Let me put my CPA hat on for a minute. When clients come to me to have their tax returns done, they don't pay me up front for ten years' worth of tax preparation. That would be silly. In reality, they make a judgment that they would like to use my services. I do the work and present them with an invoice for one year's worth of tax services. After the transaction is complete, they make a decision in their minds if the service I provided was worth the money they paid.

Of course, I understand this too. I realize I'm working for more than just one year's worth of payments. I'm trying to win clients for a lifetime – that's good business and good for the client. I work really hard trying to impress them, so they will come back another year. And even better, tell all their friends.

If I did a great job they'll be back. Every year I have to keep providing superior service and getting better. I need to know all the rules and add value to the relationship. Eventually I'll be paid for ten or more years' worth of tax returns because they'll become clients for life.

It's the Golden Rule of Business – treat your clients the same way you'd like to be treated yourself. And you'll create a following of loyal fans. The client and the advisor both win.

This balance is really important for folks who want to plan and live successfully in retirement.

Rule 10

They really should be your golden years!

Go confidently in the direction of your dreams! Live the life you've imagined. As you simplify your life, the laws of the universe will be simpler.
- Henry David Thoreau

As a financial planner, I find no greater joy than running the numbers for a client and enthusiastically proclaiming that they can take that long-awaited Hawaiian vacation with plenty of financial room to spare.

And they actually do it!

Or they can help their kids with the down payment on a first house and they report back with stories of their first overnight stay. They're almost giddy.

Stories like these are almost always the result of planning ahead for a successful retirement. It isn't just happenstance or good luck.

Three phases of retirement

As I watch my clients during their retirement, they seem to move through phases - kind of like teenagers. First, there are the "go-go" years of their sixties and sometimes well in their seventies. In this period, travel and hobbies are really important. They want to see their grandchildren as much as possible, so they attend ball games, plays and other events. It is a very social and outgoing time of life.

Next, they transition into the "slow-go" retirement years. Life is still very enjoyable, but their desire to travel diminishes. Their minds are still active and sharp, but they just don't get around like they used to. They spend less money on big-ticket items like motor homes, around-the-world cruises and home remodeling. They're more content with life's simpler pleasures. They play bridge, read the books they've put off for years, go out to dinner with friends and have their grandchildren visit them for quiet weekends.

Finally, they move into the "no-go" years. Their minds and bodies may be slowing down, so they need a little help. Perhaps they move in with their children or into a retirement community. A lot of their friends are passing away, so they really begin to understand their mortality. They enjoy company, but find themselves spending a good deal of time in quiet reflection. Sometimes they may seem lonely, but most often they're simply happy to still have time on this earth.

Do what you love while you still can.
One of my favorite client couples just loves to ski. For years they would go out to Colorado on multiple trips a year. Their faces were always tanned and smiling when they told me about their trips. They enjoyed going on ski trips with their grandchildren the most. The ski trips are a little less frequent nowadays, but they still go.

Over the years, I have watched the normal progression of my clients as they age; I can just about predict how this couple's lifestyle will change. They'll spend more time with grandchildren and at local ball games; less time on the ski slopes. I don't know when the "no-go" years will occur, but they will come. Life is a natural progression and can be a beautiful journey.

This is not a negative process – it's life.
The trick to a successful retirement is to understand these phases and enjoy each one as much as you can. In your "go-go" years, you shouldn't be so worried about potential costs in later years that you don't take that cruise to Alaska. In your "slow-go" years, you shouldn't feel like you have to sell the house you've lived in for

30 years to pay for your medical expenses. And of course, you should be able to live your "no-go" years with dignity.

To make this happen, you need to have a solid financial plan that includes the right combination of investments and insurances. You know it's the right combination when you're not constantly second-guessing yourself. You're achieving your goals, but still living within your means.

They say life is too short not to enjoy it everyday. I also believe that retirement is too long not to plan for many years of success!

They call them golden years for good reason!

Rule 11
Don't let your kids derail your retirement plans!

Parents can only give good advice or put them on the right paths, but the final forming of a person's character lies in their own hands.
- Anne Frank

As parents, we love our children and would typically do most anything to help them out. That's natural! After all, we spend a couple of decades raising and nurturing our children. But it seems like there is always one child in every family who is not very good with money. It burns a hole in their pockets.

Some families affectionately call this "financially-challenged" child the black sheep. This term is not meant to be a slap in the face. The black sheep is loved as much as any other member of the family; they just test your patience. I'm amazed at how often this situation repeats itself in so many families I meet.

Should you support a lifestyle that may be greater than your own? Single mothers and widows can be the most vulnerable. It seems like it is part of their DNA to be overly loving and nurturing. They just can't find it in their hearts to say no. They are truly saints.

I've had widowed clients with plenty of money for retirement, but their kids end up jeopardizing their mother's retirement. They have adult children who just can't seem to find the right job or go on wild spending sprees and mom is always there to bail them out. I've even had kids set up meetings with me to get more money from their mothers. They show up in nicer cars and wearing nicer clothes than their mothers ever had.

Just recently, I had a widow call who wanted to cash out her entire IRA and pay taxes at an extremely high rate. She wanted to buy her daughter a house because the daughter was going through a nasty divorce. There were two grandchildren in the picture and she just couldn't bear the thought of them living in an apartment.

It was a tough, but not dire, situation. The daughter had a good job. She was in line for a property settlement and child support. But her mother wanted to make sure her standard of living wasn't going to suffer. I asked my client what burdens she had to bear early in her life. Believe me; she had it a lot tougher. When we were done discussing her situation, she was able to put her desire to help her daughter and grandchildren in proper perspective. She didn't needlessly risk her retirement nest egg.

It's okay to cut them off!
It's okay to help a struggling child get back on their feet, but some kids are repeat offenders. They don't know when to stop asking for help. Their inability to handle their own finances means they have no understanding of how their actions are affecting their parents' retirement nest egg. I've seen this situation devastate well-planned retirements and take parents straight to the poor house.

There is an old adage that goes something like this, "If you give a man a fish you feed him for a day, but if you teach him how to fish you feed him for a lifetime." Often I see parents just keep giving their adult children fish over and over again; they don't help them fix the underlying problem. If you have a black sheep who needs financial help, you would be much better off paying for him or her to sit down with a credit counselor or a financial planner.

Sometimes finances are only a symptom of a bigger problem. If this is the case, find a specialist. Don't let a problem you're ill-equipped to handle derail the enjoyment of decades of hard work.

Living successfully in retirement means you need to take control over those things you truly control. You have to let go of the stuff you don't control. Letting go is tough when you're considering the life of someone for whom you care deeply, but your own emotional health is an important part of a long life.

Life is not harder today for your kids than it was for you when you were growing up. You made it, didn't you?

Rule 12
Your IRA can be a powerful tool!

Consumers are at risk of falling into the IRA accumulation trap where their retirement funds are lost to needless and excessive taxation. Consumers need to work with advisors who are IRA distribution specialist, and less than 1% are.
– Ed Slot

Many retirees or soon-to-be-retirees have a lot of money in their IRA accounts. The need for IRA and retirement plan savings has long been drilled into the heads of business owners, captains of industry and working-class Americans alike. The government has offered tax benefits and employers have implemented retirement plans.

Although much of the money in IRAs comes from years of individual IRA deposits, most of it tends to come from rollovers. The biggest sources of rollovers are usually contributions made to 401(k) plans. These balances tend to grow quickly when you consider the initial tax savings, possible employer contributions and years of deferred income taxes on the earnings.

Overall, this has been a good thing! I've seen ordinary folks who never thought they would be millionaires retire with seven-figure balances in their 401(k) accounts — all the result of years of steady savings. Planning ahead and sticking to your plan is critical to a successful retirement.

Can your IRA be TOO big?

Once retired, many folks have rolled over a lifetime of savings into their IRA accounts. They may have small balances in savings accounts, a few outside investments and a lot of equity in their homes, but the biggest chunk of their retirement nest egg is in an IRA. The good news is that IRAs can give you a secure retirement cash flow, but they can also be full of tax issues and traps.

The first thing to realize is that the money in your IRA, even though it has your name on it, may not really be all yours. Uncle Sam has a tax mortgage and he wants to be paid back for all the tax savings he gave you over the years. Your net worth might not be as high as you might think because of this possible tax liability.

But remember, the benefits of these tax-advantaged savings tools were well worth it. Don't use a potential tax mortgage as an excuse to avoid IRA and 401(k) contributions. Tax deferral, putting taxes off into the future, allows your money to work longer and harder. One way to think about it is that taxes paid in the future are usually less expensive than taxes today or in the past.

The IRA trick

The trick becomes looking for ways to make sure more of your IRA money stays in your pocket and keep it out of Uncle Sam's wallet. Learned Hand, a famous American judge, once said, "Anyone may so arrange his affairs that his taxes shall be as low as possible. He is not bound to choose that pattern which will best pay the Treasury."

Most folks know that money withdrawn from an IRA prior to age 59 ½ is subject to a tax penalty. They may also know that by age 70½ they are required to begin Required Minimum Distributions (RMD). But there is more to IRA tax planning than just these two commonly-understood rules.

Tax planning, particularly when it relates to IRA and rollover accounts, is a critical element of a successful retirement. This planning needs to start with your decisions about which retirement savings tools to use and continue through the way you pass any balances on to your heirs. Many of the biggest mistakes I see being made in retirement planning today surround improper interpretation of IRA rules and regulations.

Unfortunately, I've seen example after example of folks not understanding the rules surrounding IRAs. When they change jobs they cash in their 401(k) plans to pay bills instead of rolling them into IRAs. They end up with a tax bill for about 40 percent of the amount they've already spent. Sometimes people spend money from their IRA without thinking about their tax bracket or potential penalties. IRA rules are complicated. When it comes to the tax laws the old adage, "Don't try this at home," definitely applies.

For example, if you retire between ages 60 and 65, you'll most likely be in a lower tax bracket than you were when you were working; especially if you delay drawing your Social Security payments. One easy-to-implement idea that many folks miss is pulling money out of your traditional IRAs during this low tax period. Even better, you may be able to convert some or all of this money to a tax-free Roth IRA. Not only would you be paying taxes at a lower rate than when you were working; you would have greater control over your taxes when you are required to start taking withdrawals at age 70½.

The benefit of wearing 2 hats...

I have always felt that your investment planning

should be coordinated with your tax planning. That's why I wear both hats. As a professional schooled in both investment management and tax preparation, I can more easily look at my clients' retirement needs from both angles.

Most investment advisors don't understand taxes deeply; they know the basics but they typically don't have someone with a CPA license and a master's degree in taxes on staff. The same is also true with tax professionals; they can be very technical folks but they're concerned with following the rules, not making your investments stretch. If you don't have an advisor with expertise in both fields, your job will be to coordinate the efforts of your investment manager and tax planner.

Stretching your IRA to build your legacy.
Although I'm trying not to be too technical in this book, there is one additional IRA strategy to mention – stretching your IRA. Many, many mistakes are being made in this area. They are mistakes that could last several lifetimes.

Your first priority with your IRA in retirement will most likely be to use it to generate current income. But given the large size of many IRAs today, it will probably last longer than just your living years. So when you pass away, you will be leaving some of your IRA money to your family. Normally, you would pass it onto your spouse and when she dies it will go to your kids.

At this point, if your beneficiary forms are not written correctly, your kids will have to take the money out of the IRA over just five years. This has the potential for creating some rather large tax bills. A lot of your hard-earned IRA will be wasted on taxes; particularly if your kids have high-paying jobs.

On the flipside, if you set things up correctly, your kids will have the option of taking the money out of your IRA more slowly. They can "stretch" it over their entire lifetimes. The longer they have to pay Uncle Sam, the more the money will grow, and the more total payments they will receive.

Each and every year they will get a check from you. That's right! The check will come from your IRA account and your name will still be on it. What a great legacy! When you're sitting on a puffy cloud in the sky, you can look down on your kids (or even your grandkids) and watch them continue to enjoy the benefits of your lifetime of hard work.

Don't take your IRA for granted.
IRAs and rollovers have become almost commonplace, but they shouldn't be taken for granted. There's more to managing your IRA than deciding if you own the right mutual funds. After all, IRAs tend to be one of the largest assets of folks planning and living successfully in retirement. A small mistake in IRA planning can undo a lifetime of planning.

Specialized IRA Training

I have personally joined Ed Slott's Elite IRA Advisor Group. Through this program I regularly attend conferences on the specialized rules surrounding IRAs and receive additional knowledge through newsletter and conference call updates. According to Mr. Slott, "The average advisor is not an IRA distribution specialist and cannot competently address these issues. In fact much less than 1% are." More information can be found at www.irahelp.com.

Rule 13

Taxes, taxes, and more taxes...

Be thankful we're not getting all the government we're paying for.
- Will Rogers

The taxpayer - that's someone who works for the federal government but doesn't have to take the civil service examination.
-Ronald Reagan

I have had folks come to me and say something like, "I thought when you hit age 70 you stopped paying taxes." Sorry, there is no such rule. There are a lot of people over age 70 who don't pay taxes, but that's because they have a very low taxable income.

Keeping your taxes low (or maybe even eliminating them) should be a goal for living successfully in retirement, but your first concern should be your after-tax cash flow and net worth. After all, the amount of money you can actually spend is extremely important. Keeping your taxes low makes a difference, but don't let the tail wag the dog. Don't let your obsession with taxes take away from your total financial plan.

Tax rates are like a ladder.
Think of tax rates like a ladder. Any income that you earn when you're on the ground isn't taxed. On the first and second income rungs you pay taxes at rates of 10 percent and 15 percent; these are the lowest rates. When your income moves to the third rung of the ladder; your tax rate on this increased income jumps all the way up to 25 percent. Above this rung are tax rates of 28, 33 and 35 percent.

Moving up a rung doesn't mean all of your income is taxed at your highest rate. You still pay taxes at the lower rates for income levels that fall below each rung. In reality, most people pay what we call a "blended" rate, sort of like an average of the rates for all the rungs you cross.

Some people think that if they get a raise at work or if they have additional income in retirement they could end up with less money in their pockets. That's not the way the system works. If you already make enough money to be taxed at zero percent, 10 percent, 15 percent and 25 percent, the fact that you're creeping into the 28 percent bracket doesn't change the money that's being taxed on the lower rungs of your ladder. It only affects the income on your new rung.

More income is still more income even though Uncle Sam wants more of it as your income grows. You will never have less by making more. You might however lose your motivation to make more money if it's going to be taxed at 35% and higher rates. We all have our limits.

Timing your income
Personal income can vary from year to year. Maybe a salesman makes a big commission one year and makes very little the next year. Maybe a farmer stores grain one year and sells two crops' worth the next. After you retire, you might have a large capital gain from a land sale in one year and no land sale the next.

You need to think about your average tax rate over a long period of time. If you constantly have a high year followed by a low year, you'll pay more in taxes in the high years than you save in the low years. As a tax planner, I try to match high expenses with high income years. Plus, you can sometimes accelerate legitimate expenses and defer income into later years. Tax planning is critical, especially when your income is variable.

Do you like vertical or horizontal stripes?
Sometimes clients come into my office and give

me a wink and a nudge from their elbow. They are trying to hide income or take some deductions that they can't explain with a straight face. It seems like they want to do something that deep down they know isn't right and they want a CPA's blessing.

Listen, my first name isn't Father and I don't have a confessional booth. Of course, I want to help them find all the legitimate ways possible to lower their taxes. But some of their concocted stories are really easy to dispel. Their attempts to avoid taxes stick out like a sore thumb.

The only response I can give them is this: "I really don't know the answer to your question. Ask that fellow wearing the striped suit in the cell block next to you."

Then after I have their attention, I instruct them on the hundreds of legitimate ways to accomplish their goals. And the good thing about taking the right path is that they won't be looking over their shoulder for years to come. The IRS auditor is much less likely to call.

A commercial for Capital Gains taxes

Some people rush into my office scared about a potential capital gains tax they might have to pay. They don't mind paying income taxes, but they certainly don't want to pay that dreaded capital gains tax. I have to explain that capital gains is your friend. I spend a lot of time trying to move income from ordinary income tax rates into capital gain tax rates.

Capital gains rates from your investments receive a special rate that replaces the other rates mentioned above. If you are in the 15% bracket or lower, the capital gains rate is currently 5%. If you are in a higher bracket, the capital gains rate is capped at 15%.

One way to convert ordinary income tax rates into capital gains rates is to move investments that are earning normal interest income (like CDs) into stocks. The dividends from stocks and the gains they produce when they go up in value receive lower capital gains tax treatment. So, not only do you make more money over the long haul, but you pay less in taxes.

Taxing your Social Security income
When you work, you're forced to put money into the Social Security system; it's like a tax. Your paycheck is socked each and every month. The only good thing about paying this tax is the opportunity you may have to get it back when you retire. Unfortunately, tax laws make this more difficult than it should be. The government can actually tax the benefits you worked hard to earn.

To keep things simple I will only discuss the rules for married couples. Our Social Security tax rules

are one the finest examples of our tax-writing
bureaucrats at work. It is way too complicated!

It goes something like this… Take all of your
income and add it up, including your tax-free
income. (You do get to take some of your tax
adjustments to offset this amount.) Add to this
amount one-half of your Social Security benefits
and compare this amount to $32,000. If the result
is below $32,000, you don't owe any taxes on your
Social Security Benefits. If you exceed $32,000,
you're taxed on 50% of the excess over $32,000.
You use this tax formula until your total exceeds
$45,000. At this point, you're taxed on 85% of the
excess over $45,000. After you know how much
income is being taxed by this formula, you will pay
taxes based on your tax bracket. By the way, the
government thinks they are generous; they won't
tax more than 85% of your total benefit.

Some people think it's unfair that the government
takes taxes on your Social Security payments. I'm
not going to argue with you on that one. The
system probably needs to be overhauled.

The taxation of Social Security benefits is a tricky
topic. Make sure you have a qualified CPA help
you with your planning. This is especially true
when your income is near the $32,000 or $45,000
levels. These are the danger zones where your tax
bracket can make big leaps.

Don't get carried away with deductions.
This brings me to the flip side of this conversation. By themselves, tax deductions are not meant to return all of the money you've paid in income taxes. They offset your income, not the taxes you've paid. Some folks think write-offs make things free – they don't. They actually just lower your taxable income and save taxes at whatever bracket you happen to fall in.

Think of tax deductions like coupons. If you have a coupon for something you're buying, you get a discount. It's cheaper, but it's not free. There is an old joke in which a wife comes home from the department store proclaiming she has saved her husband hundreds of dollars because of all the bargains she purchased. He quickly replies that it won't feel like such a bargain when he's paying her credit card bill. Well, the money is still gone, it is just less than it would have been.

I have seen a few clients become obsessed with paying little or no taxes. They're convinced everything is a potential tax write-off. They take their quest for deductions too far. They spend so much money on deductions that they don't have any cash left. As you plan your retirement, think of taxes as an expense you don't enjoy paying. Try to minimize them, but don't get carried away.

Tax-saving strategies are not one size fits all
A few years ago a client called to ask my opinion

on a tax shelter his neighbor bought to capture a big deduction. He figured that if his neighbor was going to save $10,000 on his taxes; he would save at least a few thousand bucks if he bought the same shelter. He was going to borrow money to invest in this highly complex program. But there was a problem; no matter how much money my client put into this tax shelter he wouldn't qualify for any deductions. His tax situation was very different.

Tax saving strategies, even something as simple as tax free bonds, might make good sense at one tax level but not at a lower level. The income on tax-free bonds avoids taxation, but these bonds also pay lower interest rates. You have to give up some interest in order to save taxes. Sometimes it's worth it and sometimes it is not.

The key to investing in bonds is to determine how much money you'll have after you pay taxes on the earnings. If you're in a high tax bracket, accepting lower interest rates and not paying taxes on the income may make a lot of sense. But if you're in a lower tax bracket, it may make more sense to earn a higher interest rate and pay taxes.

I have even seen folks put all of their money in tax-free bonds just so they could pay zero taxes. They do this even though they are in the lowest tax brackets. They're cutting off their nose to spite their face. Paying no taxes doesn't always mean you'll put more money in your pocket.

Tax-free bonds may make good sense in the 25 percent tax bracket, but if you were to place too much money in these investments your income could fall to the 15% bracket. At this lower tax level, these bonds may no longer make sense for your portfolio. You can have too much of a good thing.

A few lessons learned...
Using only one tax-saving strategy is probably not a good thing. I would love to eat chocolate ice cream for my entire diet, but I probably would be better off with some fruits and vegetables. So if you place all your money into tax-free bonds, tax-deferred annuities, tax-advantaged life insurance or a huge tax shelter; it's mostly likely a mistake.

It's also a mistake not to use up your lower tax brackets each year, especially if you're pushing your income into a higher bracket in the following year. In other words, paying more taxes this year at a 15 percent rate is a lot cheaper than paying taxes on the same income next year at a 25 percent rate. Your CPA should look at your income over a number of years to make sure you're in the lowest brackets possible over time.

I don't enjoy paying taxes or having my clients pay taxes, but my first concern is maximizing my clients' net worth. Sometimes the wisest strategy is to pay some taxes today to avoid higher taxes tomorrow. Taxes need to be managed as carefully as your investments. If not, you'll waste a lot of money that you'll never get back.

Work with a knowledgeable tax advisor. I'm biased, of course, but I feel working with a skilled CPA is money well spent. Any good advisor should be able to demonstrate that he adds value many times over what you pay him for the advice.

Good tax planning is an essential component of enjoying a successful retirement.

Rule 14
Death is unavoidable, you need an estate plan!

But in this world nothing can be said to be certain, except death and taxes.
- Benjamin Franklin

I am always shocked by the number of people who haven't taken the time to create a simple estate plan. A lot of people don't even have wills. It's like they think they'll never die. They work their lifetimes to accumulate their wealth and they're willing to ignore what will happen if they die. For most folks this doesn't need to be a complicated process.

Everybody needs a will.
Basic wills are not all that difficult. My advice is like the "Nike" commercial – "Just Do It." But don't do it yourself, hire an experienced attorney.

If your total net worth is less than two million dollars (or you are young) and you don't own any complicated businesses or investments, a basic "I love you" will usually be adequate. This is the kind of will I'm currently using for my estate. I simply give all my assets to my wife so she can continue to stay home and raise my kids if something happens to me. For the moment I want to keep life as simple for her and our kids as possible. As I get older and my net worth grows, I'll probably add a few more wrinkles. I've reviewed my will with my attorney.

Everybody needs a power-of-attorney.
A power-of-attorney form for both financial matters and healthcare matters is just as important as a will. When my mother was sick, I was able to take her power-of-attorney into her bank and transact business on her behalf. I could pay her bills, make arrangements at the nursing home, and collect all of her mail. Without this simple piece of paper, life would have been a lot more difficult. An attorney can explain the process to you better than I can, but I have to tell you it made all the difference in the world. You also need a medical power-of-attorney for healthcare reasons. This way, people you trust can make an appropriate decision on your behalf if you become incapacitated.

Do you need a trust?
This discussion can become complex very quickly,

so I will only highlight a few important facts. You need to sit down with an attorney who specializes in estate planning to make the best decisions for your situation.

You probably want to consider a trust in addition to a will if one of the following situations exists:

1. You have property in multiple states – this will avoid probate in each and every state, which can be expensive.
2. You want to take care of children from a prior marriage. For example, you may want to give your current spouse an income from your investments for the rest of their life, but then you would like the money to go to your kids, not your spouse's kids.
3. You have children who are not responsible with money.
4. Your assets, including the proceeds from life insurance, will exceed two million dollars.
5. You have a big IRA and you would like to ensure that your heirs stretch out the payments over a long period of time for maximum value and minimum taxes.
6. You have heirs with special needs, or who are minors.

If you answered yes to any of the questions above, you should sit down with your lawyer to discuss the use of a trust. Next, let's look at some trust basics.

What is a living trust?

The use of living trusts has become somewhat common. Basically, this type of trust will replace your will as the governing document if you die or become incapacitated. Most living trusts are revocable, which means you can get out of the trust at any time prior to death or incapacity. Because you can change your mind at any time and control the money in the trust, you still pay income taxes on the earnings of the trust. People get confused about taxes and trusts. You don't save any income taxes with a revocable trust; you might save some estate taxes which I will discuss below in the more complex trust section.

With a revocable living trust, you generally act as your own trustee while you're still alive. In the case of a couple, upon the first person's death (say the husband's) there is no probate and the wife mostly likely becomes the trustee. When the wife dies there is still no probate, but the couple's personal representative will need to sit down with an attorney and distribute the assets from the trust. At this point, the personal representative will most likely dissolve the trust, unless it has a continuing purpose.

One of the biggest benefits of this type of trust is the ease in which assets transfer to your beneficiaries when you die. Plus, you avoid the cost of probate. Instead, you pay an attorney to set up the trust. This will typically cost more than a will but less than probate. You also pay an attorney upon the second death to assist with the dissolution.

Back to wills for a couple of minutes

Let me give you some reasons that you would still consider having a will. Wills are simple and don't require putting your money in trust while you're alive. They're typically very affordable – a few hundreds of dollars, not a few thousands of dollars. You simply have a written document that tells a judge where your assets should go when you die.

A lot of people become overly concerned that their attorney is going to make a bundle in probate fees when they die. In Iowa for example, the law allows the attorney fees to be up to two percent of the value of your estate. If you have a big estate, your heirs could end up with a huge legal fee. Two percent is the maximum allowed, but you and your executor have the right to negotiate with your attorney. Remember, everyone deserves to be paid a fair amount for their services. You'll just need to shop for the right attorney who charges a reasonable fee.

If you die with a will in place, your assets will go through probate. This process may take some extra time, but this could be a good thing. Your heirs end up with court supervision. A judge will have the job of making sure the right people get

your assets. Oftentimes, there are unclear title issues with land and houses. The probate process makes sure that your heirs receive a clear title.

A will can also be helpful if you have minor children. It gives you a chance to name a guardian, so your children are taken care of when you die. If a minor child will inherit some of your assets, the court will be able to supervise how the money is invested and spent. This is called a conservatorship and it can be a hassle. This concern is probably best solved with a trust.

Do I really pay taxes when I die?

The short answer is "no." You won't be around, so your heirs will pay any taxes that are due (using your money of course). Currently the estate tax applies only if you die with more than $2,000,000 in assets. The first $2,000,000 is exempt from tax. This will include any life insurance proceeds that are paid.

To illustrate, let's say a husband and wife have $3,000,000. With the typical will, the husband will leave everything that's in his name to his wife when he dies. In the case of a married couple, there is a special rule that says money transferred between spouses is not subject to any estate taxes. This means that when the husband dies and leaves all of his assets to his wife there is no tax.

Here's where it gets tricky. At this point, if the wife dies, she'll have $3,000,000 or more worth of

assets in her name. But only the first $2,000,000 will be exempt from estate taxes. Anything over $2,000,000 will be taxed at 45 percent. In this example, the taxes due would be at least $450,000. It's an enormous tax bill, especially when you consider that you've probably paid income taxes on that money when you earned it.

Be careful, the tax laws change every year. You need to double check the limits and tax amounts for the year that you plan to die (only kidding......sort of).

How to avoid $450,000 in taxes
Let's look at one more type of trust, a credit-shelter trust. Sometimes called an A-B trust, a credit-shelter trust is a simple technique for avoiding estate taxes. It's basically a plan you put together while you and your spouse are both alive that helps makes sure you minimize your estate taxes; particularly after the death of the second spouse.

In the example above, if the husband leaves a portion of his assets to a credit-shelter trust instead of to his wife, the family would avoid paying taxes on the wife's death. When the husband dies as much as $2,000,000 of his assets could go into a credit-shelter trust and the rest could go to his wife. The amount placed in trust would use up his estate tax exemption and would never be subject to estate taxes. By not using a trust in the first example, they basically gave away the husband's exemption.

With a credit-shelter trust the wife could still have all the income from the trust and any principal if she needs it, so it's just like it's her money. But the money the husband put into trust would not be subject to estate tax when she dies. Her estate would only be around $1,000,000 and it would be free from taxes too. The family would avoid $450,000 or more in estate taxes.

This may seem kind of complicated, but it's really pretty straightforward. Whenever I see this potential problem brewing in one of my client's estates, I send them to an attorney. I like the idea of helping my clients save hundreds of thousands of dollars in taxes. Besides, paying a few thousand dollars in attorney's fees today is a lot better than paying $450,000 in taxes later.

Everybody's going to die...
That's about all I'm going to dig into trusts and wills in this writing. The bottom line is that you can't afford not to have a sound estate plan. Planning your estate is an essential element of living successfully in retirement. A good plan will save you and your family time, money, hassles and taxes. I strongly believe in having my clients meet with a good attorney.

No Estate Plan

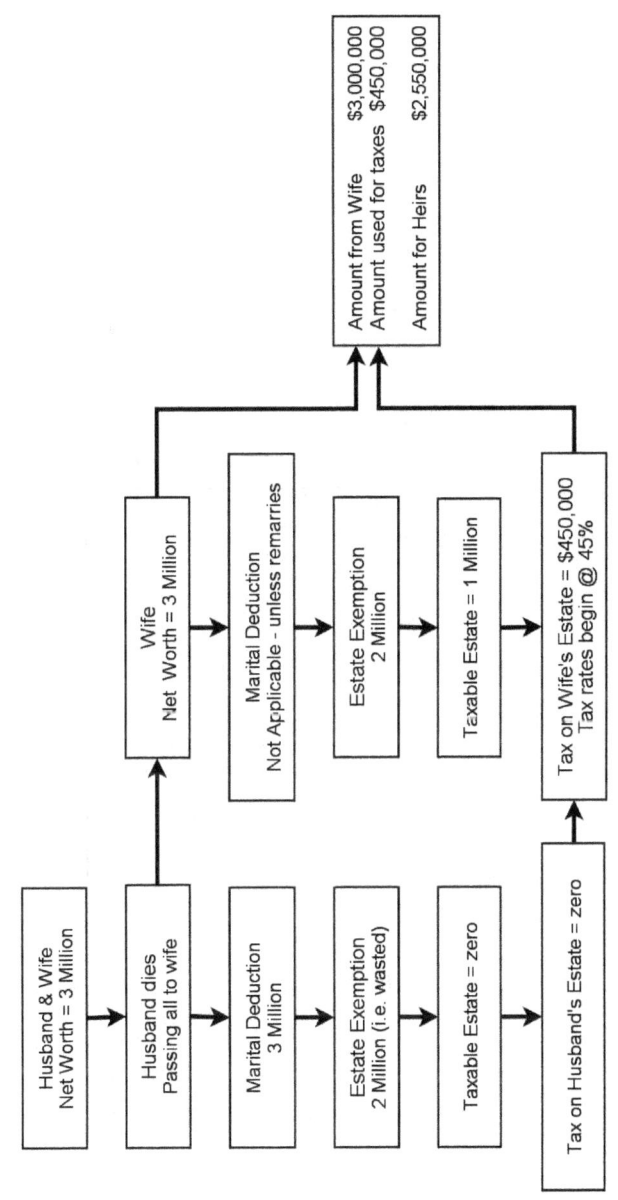

Husband & Wife Net Worth = 3 Million

↓

Husband dies Passing all to wife

↓

Marital Deduction 3 Million

↓

Estate Exemption 2 Million (i.e. wasted)

↓

Taxable Estate = zero

↓

Tax on Husband's Estate = zero

↓

Wife Net Worth = 3 Million

↓

Marital Deduction Not Applicable - unless remarries

↓

Estate Exemption 2 Million

↓

Taxable Estate = 1 Million

↓

Tax on Wife's Estate = $450,000 Tax rates begin @ 45%

Amount from Wife	$3,000,000
Amount used for taxes	$450,000
Amount for Heirs	$2,550,000

111

Simple First Step Estate Plan

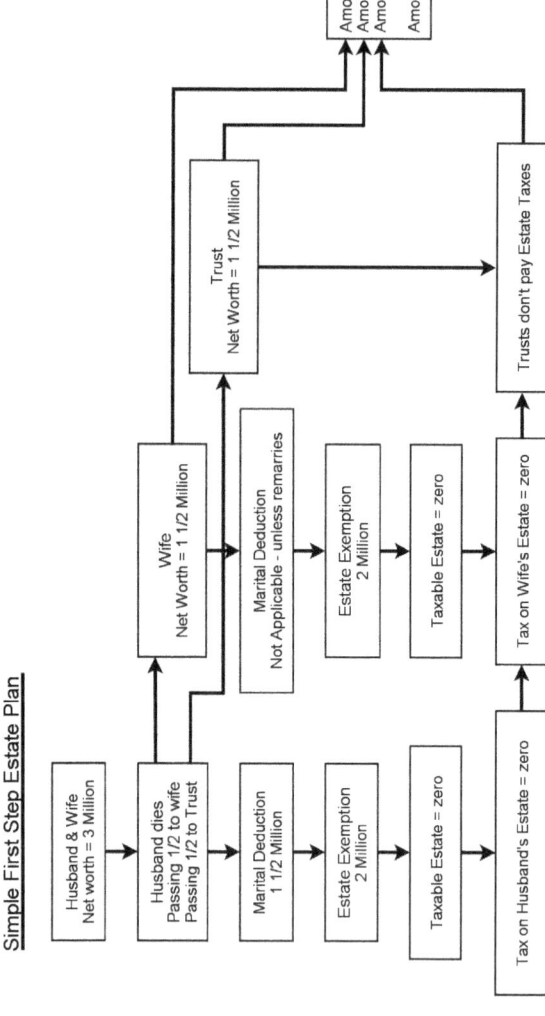

Amount from Wife	$1,500,000
Amount from Trust	$1,500,000
Amount used for taxes	0
Amount for Heirs	$3,000,000

Husband & Wife
Net worth = 3 Million

Husband dies
Passing 1/2 to wife
Passing 1/2 to Trust

Wife
Net Worth = 1 1/2 Million

Trust
Net Worth = 1 1/2 Million

Marital Deduction
1 1/2 Million

Marital Deduction
Not Applicable - unless remarries

Estate Exemption
2 Million

Estate Exemption
2 Million

Taxable Estate = zero

Taxable Estate = zero

Tax on Husband's Estate = zero

Tax on Wife's Estate = zero

Trusts don't pay Estate Taxes

Note:
Estate Exemption is 2 million in 2007 & 2008.
Exemption changes to 3 1/2 million in 2009.
Exemption is unlimited in 2010 - i.e. die in this year and there is no tax.
Exemption changes to 1 million in 2011 and the rate is 55%.

Future tax law creators are being required to choose between the rules in force in 2009, 2010 and 2011.
Although opinions vary widely, there is strong reason to believe that the 2009 rule will prevail (i.e. exemption of 3 1/2 million).

Rule 15
Dust off your life insurance policies — please!

There are worse things in life than death. Have you ever spent an evening with an insurance salesman?
- Woody Allen

You need to create three financial plans. The first one should be for you and your spouse together. Hopefully, this is the one you both get to enjoy! This is the one where you have hobbies, enjoy time together and maybe even travel often – your ideal retirement.

You should also have two additional plans that account for the possibility of a premature death. I know the thought of losing your spouse is not easy to think about. But refusing to consider this possibility doesn't reduce the odds of it happening. So, you might as well be prepared.

In my work as a financial planner, one of the most devastating meetings I can have is with the spouse of a recent retiree who passed away unexpectedly. Because women statistically live longer than men, it's usually with a widow. Suddenly, all the couple's retirement dreams have ended before they had a chance to enjoy it. The surviving spouse is left to pick up all the pieces. It's not easy, but it's a lot less painful when proper planning has been done.

A widow's tears
All too often I get to experience a widow's tears. Sometimes it's difficult to determine if she's crying over the loss of her husband or crying over her financial circumstances. I know this sounds terribly cold, but it happens! The grief that comes with the loss of a lifelong companion can be multiplied by being financially unprepared. Half of the husband's pension may be lost, Social Security income shrinks, there's inadequate savings and no life insurance to fill the gaps.

If you do nothing else as a result of reading this chapter; dust off your life insurance polices. Make sure you understand what you own and how they will work if something happens to you or your spouse. If you're confused at all, meet with your financial advisor to conduct a complete review.

Life insurance can be an important element of your second and third financial plans. When it's properly structured, life insurance can help you pay expenses related to a premature death, cover estate taxes and generate ongoing income for the surviving spouse. Life insurance cannot be ignored if you want to enjoy a successful retirement.

Although I don't sell life insurance, I do take the time to help my clients review their insurance polices and needs. It's part of our ongoing planning process. Think of it this way; if I help my clients minimize their taxes and allocate their assets, but ignore the pitfalls of a premature death - I'm not doing my job. All of my good work could be undone by an untimely death.

There are a lot of opinions on the best types of life insurance policies, the correct way to own them, how to name your beneficiaries and which bells and whistles are truly valuable. Avoid slick salesmen who only want a commission. If your trusted advisor doesn't understand life insurance, get him or her to point you to somebody who does. Don't be afraid to dig under the hood and make the right decision for all three of your financial plans.

Separate life insurance and investment decisions

I'm of the mindset that you should not mix your life insurance needs with your investment desires. The expenses on the investments inside an insurance policy are typically way too high. Plus, insurance policies are not very liquid if you change your mind or need the money for something else. And most of the contracts are too hard to comprehend.

Some so-called planners who work for life insurance companies suggest you place all your assets into a life insurance contract when you retire. During retirement, you're supposed to take tax-free loans from the policy for income. Of course, you have to pay the insurance company interest on the loan. When you die, the loan will be paid for from the insurance settlement.

I've never understood why anybody should pay interest on a loan to get their own money back. After you have exhausted your own money, it's true that they'll loan you money against your death benefit. But you're paying interest on the loan and you're paying insurance expenses on the investments. It's very expensive! Plus, these contracts are not very flexible once you have committed yourself.

I realize there is more than one way to skin a cat, so differing approaches are worth exploring. But I consider these insurance folks to be salesmen and not financial planners. It's funny that every answer to every financial plan they develop is to put all your money into an insurance contract!

When all you have in your toolbox is a hammer, every situation starts to look like a nail. And guess who's the nail that may get pounded – you! Use a professional who will use the entire toolbox to select the right tool for your situation. Insurance is one of the many important tools you need to consider; it just needs to be used in the right way.

Rule 16

What's all the fuss about long-term care insurance?

Experience is a hard teacher because she gives the test first, the lesson afterwards.
- Vernon Sanders Law

In my practice, I don't sell long-term care insurance, so what I'm about to tell you is completely objective. I also know that insurance makes many people nervous. Most of us are hesitant to spend money on something we don't plan on using. Plus, we don't want to get ripped off.

For the next few minutes, put these emotions aside...
One of the greatest fears for any of us is the thought of ending up in a nursing home. This is

particularly true for retirees. It's hard to picture living under constant nursing supervision as being enjoyable retirement. And we all know that the cost of nursing home care is going through the roof. In my town, the cost of a nursing home is around $50,000 a year for the most basic services.

Yet the fact remains, most people are not doing a good job planning for this looming possibility. Somehow we convince ourselves that if we refuse to think about this issue it won't happen to us. Unfortunately, the odds are fairly high that you or your spouse will spend some time needing nursing assistance. It could be a temporary stay in an assisted living facility, extended home health care or a permanent relocation.

So, let me ask you an important question: "If you had to go into a nursing home, would your spouse have enough income to live comfortably?" If your answer is "no" or "maybe not," you should consider purchasing long-term care insurance. It's just that simple.

I eat my own cooking.
Like most folks, I don't like buying insurance, but I bought a long-term care policy when I was 46. It was a stewardship issue for my wife and kids. As the breadwinner and financial decision maker in our household, I wanted to make sure we could pay the bills in the unlikely event I fell ill and required extended nursing care.

The younger you buy the insurance, the cheaper it is. I used the affordability gained by buying early to add some Cadillac-type features to my policy. First, I included a rider that will increase my benefits by five percent each year (remember the cost of inflation). Next, I designed my coverage to be paid off in ten years so my retirement living cost will be lower.

Don't count on Uncle Sam.

A common excuse for avoiding long-term care insurance is the ill-found belief that the government will take care of you if you end up in a nursing home. Actually, this is true; it's called Medicaid and it starts at the point when you only have $2,000 left in assets! To add insult to injury, the government will take your Social Security check and leave you with $30 a month for spending money. Your spouse will be able to keep the house as long as he or she is alive, but the government will make a financial claim on it. In the end, your kids will have to pay the government back before they can receive an inheritance.

When you are on Medicaid, you have to stay in a double room. The government is not going to put you up in a private suite. Unfortunately, many of the things you have to do in a nursing home are embarrassing. I spent a lot of time with my mother while she was in a nursing home and hospital; life would have been so much more pleasant in the privacy of a single room.

Also, from my experience, if you're on Medicaid you don't get your choice of nursing homes. Most homes have a limited number of beds for Medicaid patients. The government doesn't pay them as much as a private patient, so they have to be selective. This may not sound fair, but to give top-notch care, the higher quality facilities have to turn a profit. Would you want to live in a nursing home that was losing money?

You're not a piece of meat.
I don't want to cast a bad light on all nursing homes. There are some wonderful facilities staffed with the most caring of people. These folks do an unbelievable job in the most difficult of situations, with smiles on their faces. At the same time, some places are dismal, negative and smelly. Do you want to be able to have some choice in the matter?

My own mother, in her final few months, was in the process of spending her assets down. She had a long-term care policy, but it had a $100 a day limit and she was in a facility that cost $135 a day for a double room. With all her other expenses, it was looking as if we were going to need to make application for Medicaid. One day she remarked to me that she just felt like a piece of meat. People were telling her she would have to move to another nursing home, then back to the hospital and then to yet another hospital. Life can be unpleasant when you're in this situation. Try to leave your options open.

Losing control is tough.
As you get older, you begin to lose control over many of your decisions and your activities. You may be used to caring for your children; now they're helping you with the most basic things. Your doctor may decide you cannot drive. Your body won't do the things your mind tells it to do. Remembering things isn't as easy as it once was. And even the wealthiest retirees can grow anxious about their money. Long-term care insurance can stack the deck in your favor. It leaves one less thing to chance.

Sure, you feel great now; the thought of you or your spouse needing to go into a nursing home seems remote. But that's the funny thing about insurance; you have to buy it when you don't need it. Once the signs start pointing toward your possibly needing the insurance, no one is going to sell it to you. It's called being insurable; you have to buy it while you are healthy.

Rule 17
Annuities won't solve all of your retirement challenges.

You got to be very careful if you don't know where you're going, because you might not get there.
-Yogi Berra

Annuities have become very popular in retirement planning. The problems an annuity can potentially solve are appealing to a lot of folks who are planning for a successful retirement. Guaranteed income streams, protection of principal, the promise that you won't outlive your money and tax deferral are all terrific selling points. Unfortunately, a lot of the folks who push annuities are really just salesmen and don't truly understand retirement planning.

As I explain annuities further to you, I don't want to sound like I'm totally negative toward them. In truth, I sometimes use them as an investment choice for my own clients. I just want you to be able to understand the difference between sales hype and the proper use of annuities for planning or living for retirement.

Annuities can be too expensive.

First, consider the cost of owning many annuities, particularly variable and index annuities. The costs tend to be higher than more traditional investments. This added cost is usually not for investment management, it covers extra benefits that protect your principal in life and at death. After all an annuity, by its simplest definition, is a life insurance policy. If these insurance-like features are important to your financial plan, then they may be justified.

Annuities require full disclosure.

In my experience, the benefits of annuities are often overstated, the costs are understated and the details are tough to understand. This is a terrible combination when you're planning for retirement. I probably wouldn't even bring this up if I didn't see it happen over and over again.

If you're considering an annuity, you need to be able to clearly see all of the positives and negatives at one time. Legally, thanks to the fine print of the contract, all the facts are available. But this doesn't mean the folks who sell them even know what they're talking about. I don't want to cast a bad light on all annuity salesmen, but I've seen some horrible stuff. It's usually the result of poor training.

I can't count the number of times I've asked someone who owns an annuity why they bought it only to find that they didn't really know. All they can say is that it's supposed to be safe and saves taxes. When we look at what they actually own, they grimace at the details. They come up with more reasons *not* to own it than to own it, but at this point it may be too late. The penalties for getting out of some of these annuities are like highway robbery – especially some of the more commonly-sold index annuities.

You live before you die.
I recently helped evaluate a large retirement portfolio where a good portion of the assets had been placed into annuities. The woman who asked me to review her situation needed more income. Regrettably, the annuities she owned were worth a lot less than when they were initially invested. This was partially because they were purchased just before the stock market took a major downturn, but it had been at least four years and they should have fully recovered. High internal costs and poor investment management were the culprits of this continued underperformance.

The only advice the salesman who sold her the annuities could offer was to not worry about the current value. He told her to focus on the death benefit. Hello! This already-retired investor was looking for more current income. Besides, most folks I know are more concerned with using their money while they're alive; not making sure someone else gets it when they're gone.

Don't be sold.
Annuities are often sold rather than bought. Unsophisticated or poorly informed investors are talked into putting their money into annuities rather than the annuity being chosen as the best alternative from a broad spectrum of options. Annuities are complex contracts with insurance companies. In the absence of understanding what they are buying, investors too often rely on a sales pitch.

"Annuities are complex contracts" is a phrase worth repeating. If you are considering an annuity, you need to fully understand it. Check the credentials of your salesman to be sure he understands what he is saying. If you're not sure of either of these things, don't buy an annuity. There are plenty of investment alternatives and many financial advisors who understand retirement planning.

Annuities come in many flavors.
There are several types of annuities. Let's look at a few more of the more popularly-sold contracts:

Fixed annuities – Some pay a locked-in interest rate and tend to be pretty straightforward. They're called fixed annuities and on the surface they look a lot like a bank CD. You benefit from deferring taxes on the earnings (As a note of caution, please make sure that deferring taxes is something that is good for you and your heirs).

But you have to watch out for short-term teaser rates. The initial interest rate may sound good, but it may quickly go down to a guaranteed minimum amount – typically around three percent. This rate will hardly keep pace with inflation. Fixed annuities are made worse when your contract has a withdrawal penalty that extends beyond the teaser rate period. You're left holding the bag with a very low-paying investment.

Index annuities – Another type of annuity pays income based on a formula that is tied to the stock market. These annuities have become popular because many of them guarantee you that you will never lose money. In general terms, these products are called index annuities. They take away the risk of losing money in stocks, while promising some of the upside if the market goes higher. For some folks this is attractive. Others understand that stocks rarely lose money over long periods of time and are comfortable investing outside an annuity.

Unfortunately, many index annuities have a lot of hidden tricks. And the salesmen who push them don't even need to be licensed to sell investments. Be *extra* careful with index annuities. Be sure you understand how much upside you really get; some only promise 75 or 80 percent of their corresponding stock market index. Make sue you understand the internal charges; they can be grossly overpriced. Most importantly, be sure you understand how long your surrender period will last. Some index annuities tie you up with penalties that exceed 15% for periods lasting longer than 15 years.

Variable annuities – In many respects, variable annuities are much like mutual funds. The big difference is that they come with an insurance wrapper that allows you to defer taxes on the earnings. Basically, you invest your money, hold the contract for a stated period of time to avoid withdrawal penalties and defer taxes until the money is withdrawn.

Investment, administrative and insurance costs can range from slightly less than two percent to over three percent – which is high. These costs go toward death and living benefit guarantees. Although some of these expenses may be worthwhile, they can also be confusing. Tax-deferral is nice, but all income that is eventually withdrawn from an annuity is taxed at ordinary income tax rates. Alternatively, stocks and mutual funds can qualify for capital gains tax rates which can be half as much as ordinary rates.

You can't defer taxes if you wouldn't owe any taxes!

Not so long ago, a tax client of mine proudly explained that his mother hadn't filed an income tax return in years. After a few questions, I discovered that it was because she had invested all of her money in a fixed annuity that was paying her around three percent. She had owned this contract for a very long time; it had grown to over $200,000 from an original investment of just over $100,000. It seemed like a great thing; she hadn't paid pay taxes on almost $100,000 in interest.

Then we dug a little deeper...

His mother was already in a zero percent tax bracket or a very low tax bracket when she first bought the annuity. She didn't need tax deferral. This continued to be the case over all the years she owned the annuity. Remember, no taxes are due on the first $10,000 or so of income each year. Even at its current value, the annuity was only earning around $6,000. There was no tax benefit to this fixed annuity and this was the thing my client and his mother were most excited about.

It gets worse!
My client's mother is very old and in poor health.

Her son expects that she may not make it another year. What will happen to this annuity if she dies? Her only son will inherit the money and will have to pay taxes on all the earnings (around $100,000) at his nice fat tax rate of 35 percent – about $35,000 in taxes. If we were to pull the earnings out of the annuity before his mother passes away, she will have a lot of income and will also have to pay taxes at a rate of at least 15 percent – over $15,000.

Turning back the clock...

If we could go back in time and put this same money in a Certificate of Deposit (CD) that paid the same rate of interest as the annuity, my client's mother would have a similar amount of money. She wouldn't have paid any taxes because she still would have been in a zero percent tax bracket. The big difference is that, at her passing, there would be zero taxes due. By deferring taxes that didn't exist, my client's mother has unknowingly created a huge tax liability.

This is an unfortunate case that was the result of bad advice by an insurance salesman. He may have thought he was doing the right thing for this little old lady, but he didn't do his homework. He used an annuity where there wasn't a need. I can only hope he wasn't just looking for a fat commission.

Summing it all up
Annuities have become very popular product for

advisors claiming to be retirement planning specialists. In reality, they have their place. Unfortunately, a lot of the so-called advisors who push annuities are just poorly-trained salespeople. They should not be giving advice on something so important.

When used appropriately, annuities can provide a lot of benefits for folks who are planning for a successful retirement. Guaranteed income streams, protection of principal, and the promise that you won't outlive your money and tax deferral could all be terrific benefits. But oftentimes, these benefits come with strings attached. Make sure you understand the strings.

The bottom line – be careful!

Before you invest in an annuity, do your homework. Be a buyer, don't be sold. Ask yourself a few questions: Is your salesman just trying to generate a commission or does he know his stuff? Do you understand all the costs associated with the product you are buying? Are the benefits worth the costs and limitations?

Rule 18

There are two sides
to most issues —
explore them both!

Success is more a function of consistent common sense than it is of genius.
– An Wang

There are two sides to most of the issues I've covered in this book. Run as fast as you can from anyone who's offering advice but unwilling to share the downside of their recommendations. As I stated in the introduction, I'm an optimistic person. I believe folks are smart enough to understand what's best for their situation if everything is properly explained. As someone living or planning a successful retirement, you need to avoid the mumbo jumbo we financial professionals often speak.

Dare to be different.

I didn't invent the principals outlined in this book – I merely observed human behavior. I see people who are happy and content and I see people who are edgy, angry and possibly miserable. Over the years I have observed and made mental notes of what I believe to be the key differences between these two groups.

Many of the principles explained in this book may be different from the advice you hear from other advisors. That's okay! You don't have to agree with me, you just need to understand the path you're taking to enjoy your golden years.

My goal for retirement is not unlimited wealth. I believe if that is your goal, you'll never be satisfied. You'll always want more – a bigger house, longer vacations and a bunch of other stuff that really doesn't matter.

As I watch folks in their retirement years, the ones who are the happiest have defined their own levels of contentment. It includes more stuff than you can measure with dollars and cents. They're surrounded by family and friends. They're active in their communities. They always have a smile on their faces. They have arranged their financial affairs to support a standard of living with which they are most comfortable.

Simple common sense

I'm no Howard Hughes or Warren Buffet, but

then again I never set out to be. I look at things with a simple eye and use my Midwestern values to do what makes sense. I try to cut through the marketing glimmer and half-truths to do what is right for my clients. I use these same principles to manage my own finances.

As I started my own firm, I just figured that if I worked hard, served people honestly and treated everybody with respect, my business would grow. I've been very fortunate. I try to be a good steward of my own money and not waste it on interest, commissions and taxes. I don't mind paying for good service or good results, as long as I receive value in return. I don't like mindlessly wasting resources. Most of us have wasted so much that if we just stop wasting from this point forward it will all provide us with a nice retirement.

Epilogue
Summing it all up!

It takes 20 years to build a reputation and five minutes to ruin it. If you think about that, you'll do things differently.
– Warren Buffett

Never trade who you are for what you want.
– Ron Dickinson

The mission statement of my business is "**Turning your retirement dreams into reality through proven, time-tested investment solutions.**"

I am focused on a very specific goal – making your retirement be all that you dreamed it could be. We all have different goals and resources. My objective is to help you define your goals clearly and to show you how you can live your dream.

But we don't want to be foolish. My approach to managing portfolios includes wisdom that has been passed down through the ages. I watch your money as if it were my own; using solid, fundamentally-sound investment solutions.

The core values of my business can be summarized in three words: Trust, Communication and Results.

Trust – It's more than putting the client's needs first; it's something you earn. You earn it everyday. It doesn't even matter what reality is. That's not a high enough standard, what matters is what my clients perceive as the truth. So I work really hard to protect my reputation and the quality of my services.

Communication – This is about keeping people informed on how their retirement strategy will work and as the game is underway how they are doing. It's about helping people see the full picture. It's explaining the key concepts in terms that are understandable so that my clients can participate in the process.

Results – You can be a person of integrity and give honest communication, but unless you deliver the desired results the client won't reach their goals. It's about being one of the best so you can deliver the best. So your clients enjoy the retirement of their dreams.

www.ingramcontent.com/pod-product-compliance
Lightning Source LLC
Chambersburg PA
CBHW071815200526
45169CB00018B/319